Reflections on a Western Town

Reflections on a Western Town

An Oral History of

CRESTED BUTTE COLORADO

by
Kelsey Wirth

© 1996 by Oh-Be-Joyful Press
All rights reserved. Printed in the United States of America.
First Edition

Library of Congress Cataloging-in-Publication Data
Wirth, Kelsey D., 1969– .
    Reflections on a western town : an oral history of Crested
  Butte, Colorado / Kelsey D. Wirth.
      p. cm.
    Includes bibliographical references and index.
    ISBN 0-9649185-0-1 (cloth).— ISBN 0-9649185-2-8 (paper)
    1. Crested Butte (Colo.)—Social life and customs. 2. Crested
Butte (Colo.)—History.   I. Title.
F784.C797W57 1996
978.8'41—dc20
                                                          95-41750
                                                               CIP

Book Design and Typesetting: Stephen Adams
Copyediting: Sandy Fails
Proofeading: Scott Vickers
Cover Design: Stephen Adams

Oh-Be-Joyful Press
P. O. Box 804
Crested Butte, Colorado 81224

This book was written
with love and affection
for the people of Crested Butte
from the "old-timers"
whose voices recreate here
the history of the town
to the "newcomers"
who strive to preserve
its character and beauty

CONTENTS

Preface IX
Acknowledgments XIII

I. Beginnings 1

II. Mining Town 7
The Emigrants 9
The Immigrants 16
The Work 32
The Life 62

III. Snow: A Transition 83

IV. Ski Town 93
Transformation 95
The New People 110
The Power Shift 119
Recreation, Festivals, Tourists 139

V. The Challenges 149

Names and Lives 177
Dates and Facts 197
Endnotes 209
Credits 217
Index 219

PREFACE

Many people are fortunate enough to have a place that is special to them. It might be the area in which they grew up, went to school, spent time with grandparents or went on holiday with their families, or spent reunions with friends. For whatever reasons, it is a place that feels like home — somewhere, in a busy and persistently changing world, that is beautiful and familiar and full of memories for those who love it, and fills them with a sense of longing when they are not there. For me, Crested Butte has always been that place.

My parents bought an old miner's house in Crested Butte in 1971, and so I have been spending summers in Crested Butte ever since I can remember. My mother, eager to learn about her new home state of Colorado where the family had just moved, set out to drive around the Western Slope in her Volkswagen bug with two small children in the back seat. She says that when she drove into Crested Butte in May 1971, down an unpaved Elk Avenue, beneath a single strand of Christmas lights, and pulled up to the Forest Queen, she knew she had just found the most wonderful place in Colorado.

A year before, the recorded population in town was 372.[1] The largest operating coal mine in town had shut down in 1952. The ski area, which had first opened in 1962, gone into bankruptcy in 1965, and been bought in 1970 by the family that still owns it, was little known even in Colorado. Many of the people living in town had been there in the height of the coal-mining days. Since the closing of the mines, the men had found other work in Gunnison, or else spent much of their time traveling to work in other mines in the state, leaving their families behind in Crested Butte. In the summer of 1970, the "hippies" had begun to come, as word of Crested Butte spread to those who wanted to pursue an alternative lifestyle in an area that was beautiful, isolated, and affordable.[2]

As new part-time residents, my family was part of the change that had begun to occur in Crested Butte in the 1960s. And during the twenty-five years since we first came, we have seen so much more change. We were surprised to return one summer and find paved streets and a real sidewalk down Elk Avenue. The ski area on Crested Butte Mountain has developed rapidly, causing a greater seasonal influx of tourists and the building of more houses. The confines of the town have continued to expand every year. Countless stores and restaurants have come and gone, along with the waves of transient students and tourists who pass through, some settling down, but most eventually moving on.

In contrast to this constant change was the sense of permanence provided by the people who grew up in Crested Butte and made their living in the days of mining. I always knew some of the local old-timers. Johnny Krizmanich grew up with his six brothers and sisters in the little house at the corner of Fifth and Sopris which later became our home. Its small, box-like structure, sloped, uneven floors, rock and newspaper insulation in the walls, drafty windows, huge coal stove that heated the entire structure through the eight-month-long winter, and the perpetual accumulation of coal dust on everything were all memorable features of the house. Decades of discarded debris in the barn — animal traps of all sizes, horseshoes, mining tools — formed a tangible record of several lifetimes of hard work and survival.

The times I spent talking with the Krizmaniches growing up, visiting with Josephine Stajduhar next door, buying ice cream cones from Stefanic's, and accompanying my father when he went to chat with Tony Mihelich at the local Conoco station all left marked impressions on my summers spent in

Crested Butte. It was a place so different from the world where my family spent most of its time, a place which was still so remarkably connected to the past. The old-timers were the living links between the past and the present, with their melodic accents and their anecdotes about life in Crested Butte, and their very presence made the town a unique and magical place.

The Crested Butte of the past is fading quickly as there are fewer and fewer old-timers and each year brings more visitors and more homes to the hills surrounding the town. When it came time for me to choose a thesis topic in college for a bachelor's degree in American history and literature, I decided with little hesitation to do an oral history of Crested Butte. I wanted to write on a topic that had personal meaning to me, and that would be more than an academic exercise. And I knew that there were few books on Crested Butte history, and none that used personal interviews as the primary resource. Perhaps most importantly, doing an oral history project on Crested Butte would allow me to spend time with many of the same people I knew when I was growing up, and to record their stories so that they are not forgotten.

It was a privilege to have the opportunity to talk, often at great length, with the same people who intrigued me as a child and to learn from them about Crested Butte history. The people I talked to were remarkably warm and welcomed me into their homes. All were willing to talk and were very honest about growing up and living and working and raising families in Crested Butte. I was struck by the sense of dignity the people I interviewed had about their own lives, which were full of poverty and hardship but also characterized and enriched by the strength of the community in which they lived. Also remarkable was the deep sense of loss many of them have felt with the rapid pace at which the town and the surrounding area have changed and continue to change.

When I started the process of editing the text for publication, it seemed appropriate to do a series of additional interviews with people who had come to Crested Butte during the period between the late 1960s and early 1980s — people who moved to Crested Butte with the intention of skiing for just a few winters, but ended up staying and becoming permanent residents of the town. These more recent arrivals, in their devotion to the Crested Butte community and their love of the town and the surrounding area, provided a more hopeful, forward-looking view for the future of Crested Butte. Some of them also expressed fears of losing their way of life, the same way that the old-timers' way of life has gradually faded.

My hope is that this book will help preserve the voices of the old-timers, who built the community that my family found when we arrived in Crested Butte in 1971, and who still provide the town with a sense of continuity. The purpose is not to make people nostalgic for a romanticized past and wish, impossibly, to turn back the clock, but rather to explore what we can learn from both the good and the bad of Crested Butte's past. History has a way of not just telling us what once existed and where we have been, but also giving us a sense of where we want to go. As Crested Butte faces increasing challenges and pressures, the voices of the old-timers can be both our windows to the past and our guides into the future.

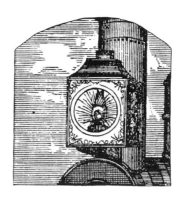

ACKNOWLEDGMENTS

Bob Johnstone served as one of my teachers in my sophomore year in college, became my advisor the following year, then kindly agreed to serve as my senior-year thesis advisor. He offered critical support of my idea of doing an oral history — which, in academic circles, is very untraditional — about a place that most people had never heard of. His sensitivity to the subject matter and editorial skills helped transform raw material into readable text.

Wren Wirth, my mother, was the driving force behind this book. Because of her sense of adventure and appreciation for beautiful places, our family came to Crested Butte almost twenty five years ago. She urged me to explore Western history in college and several years after I finished my thesis, encouraged its publication. She took on the task of collecting photographs and illustrations and coordinated the project.

Sandy Fails is a resident of Crested Butte. As editor, she helped shape the last chapter and corrected grammatical and other errors in the text. Sandy's initial read was crucial in deciding what needed to be changed or added, and her sensitivity and subtle touch provided me with important guidance.

Alice Wren Muth, my grandmother who just turned eighty, also helped with the editing. Even though she had just moved to a new home and had not yet finished unpacking, she dedicated hours of her time to painstakingly review what I had written. The text I sent her came back covered with her comments and corrections, all of which were incorporated into the final version.

Sandra Cortner took many of the photographs in this book. Crested Butte can be grateful that since moving here in the 1960s, she has taken time to record the people and events of the town. Her photographs of the old-timers are now priceless. Sandy's photography not only chronicles several decades of living history, it conveys the beauty and uniqueness of the town and its people.

Susan Anderton has created with her art work what Sandra Courtner has with her photography. Two decades ago, Susan recognized the charm of Crested Butte's barns, sheds, smokehouses and outhouses; many of those now exist only in memory and in her etchings, paintings and sketches. The town has been fortunate to have its own artist chronicling its change and reminding us why we should preserve it.

Other people helped in various ways to make this book possible. Jennifer Lloyd, Randy Udall, Gretchen Daily, Ellie Pryor, Karen Terrey, Patricia Dawson, Marcia Hegeman, Ann and Paul Ehrlich, Honeydew and Rod Nash, David Leinsdorf, Marcia Carter and Robin Hill offered advice and encouragement. Patricia Limerick, Christopher Wirth, Michelle Loy, David, Michael, Pam and Tom Green, Robin Kellogg, Jane Geniesse, and Suzanne Massie provided inspiration.

The following people helped with seeking, finding, lending, identifying, taking and developing photographs: Sue Johnson, Ed Connors, Adele Bachman, Don Bachman, Gwen and Joe Danni, Dick Eflin, Alan Hegeman, Tony Mihelich, June and Ed Rozman, Roger Rozman, Joe Saya, Rudy Sedmak, Stephanie Stokes, and Carol and Phil Yaklich. I am indebted to the Denver Public Library Western Collection, the Colorado Historical Society, the Crested Butte Historical Society, the Crested Butte Mountain Heritage Museum and to the kindness and courtesy of the people who work in those institutions, also to Gus Grosland and the Pioneer Museum in Gunnison, Ethel Rice at the Savage Library at Western State College, Michael Kraska at Colorado Fuel and Iron in Pueblo and Ann and Bernie Goldberg of Gunnison Camera Center. I thank Duane Vandenbusche for his forbearance, Dusty Demerson for his sense of adventure, Stephen Adams for his expertise, proficiency, and calm and Laurie and John McBride for the hospitality and haven of Lost Marbles Ranch.

Final thanks go to the Kindelan family who led us to the Boylan family who first told us of the glories of Crested Butte.

Reflections on a Western Town

I

BEGINNINGS

Crested Butte was first established as a supply center for the many silver-mining camps scattered about the Elk Mountains. It provided goods for the hardy and adventurous prospectors of the region who, caught up in the enthusiasm of the times, were determined to strike it rich in the mountains of the American West. The rush to the Rockies had been triggered by the discovery of gold in Cherry Creek, where Denver is today, in 1858. With territorial status in 1861 and statehood in 1876, Colorado was fast gaining national fame for its promise of great wealth and rich reward. In the frenzied search for gold and silver, prospectors crossed the Continental Divide and entered the most rugged and isolated areas of the Western Slope of the Rocky Mountains. They poured into the Gunnison area after the Brunot Treaty permanently removed the Ute Indians from that part of the state in 1873.[1]

Mining towns appeared overnight in the Elk Mountain region, with names like Gothic, Ruby-Irwin, Oh-Be-Joyful, Washington Gulch, Poverty Gulch, Pittsburg, and Elkton. The streets of Crested Butte were often lined with hundreds of mules waiting to be loaded with goods for the surrounding camps. In the winter of 1879–1880, Gunnison County was talked about all over the U.S. in newspaper stories which wildly exaggerated the richness of the area. By 1880, hordes of hopeful fortune seekers turned Gunnison into a boom town.[2] Reality did not match the hyperbole of the newspapers, however, and

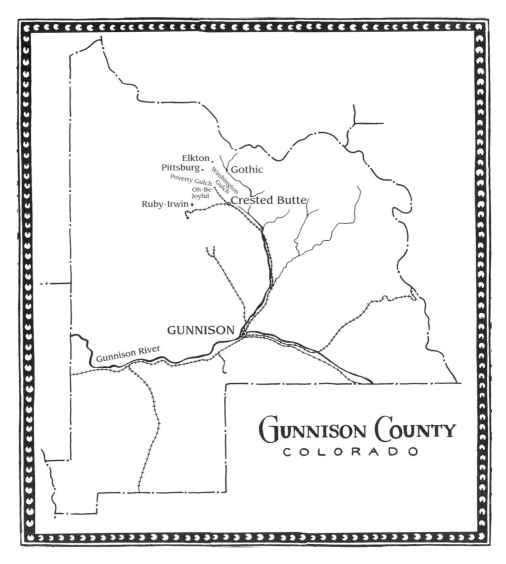

there were few success stories that met the heightened expectations of fortune. Despite its promotion and promise, the Gunnison area never experienced the boom that swept the rest of the state.[3]

Of the scores of mining settlements in Gunnison County, the town of Crested Butte was one of the few to endure. Incorporated on July 3, 1880, it took its name from the massive, 12,162-foot high peak that towers over the town, named by the Hayden Survey sent out from Harvard's Peabody Museum in 1873.[4] Unlike the numerous hard rock camps around it, Crested

Butte was not a town characterized by the romantic and enriching prospect of gold or silver. Instead, the hard reality of the dirty, dangerous, and exploitative industry of coal mining gave the town its reason for existence.

Enormous amounts of coal were being discovered in Colorado. As time went on, most of the mines were bought by railroad companies which could then fuel their trains and transport the coal to growing numbers of factories around the west. In 1880 the Denver and Rio Grande Railway Company consolidated three small coal operations into the Colorado Coal and Iron Company. Twelve years later after further mergers, the Colorado Fuel and Iron Company (CF&I) was created. It increased in size until it was the largest industry in the state with six thousand men working in twenty three mines. Several of these were in or near Crested Butte.

The story of this mining town is one of a small, predominantly immigrant community where people of different nationalities and ethnic backgrounds

A burro pack train in Gunnison, 1883

were brought together in their quest to establish a new life for themselves and their families in a strange new land. Dominated by the steel company that owned the largest mine and part of the town, and physically isolated from the rest of the world by long distances and harsh winters, the  residents led lives of simplicity and endurance in which there was little room for inflated ambitions or dreams of getting rich quick.

Much of the history of Crested Butte lies outside the romanticized, storybook images of what life in the West was like. Its past as a poor and struggling mining community also stands in striking contrast to the tourist attraction it is today. When the extraction of natural resources no longer provided economic subsistence, Crested Butte, like so many other areas in Colorado, declined sharply after World War II, until outsiders came and discovered another way to exploit its natural wealth by turning to recreation. During the last forty years, the town has undergone rapid and dramatic change with the final closing of its mines and the emergence of the ski industry and increasing numbers of summer visitors. Today, Crested Butte's economy depends on the town's identity as a destination to which urban refugees escape to fields of play and relaxation.

This is the story of the human side of the transformation. The "old-timers," who lived in both worlds, recall the changes in family and community values, the shifts in collective lifestyles, and the difficulties and challenges of the transition from old to new.

II

MINING TOWN

THE EMIGRANTS

Somebody come over here first, and of course they sent back for somebody else, and it just mushroomed. But how the first one ever came here, I don't know. In my dad's case, his dad, my grandad . . . came over with several others, and they were mining around the country, one place or another, and they decided Crested Butte was the place, so then he sent back for his wife and the two kids. They told us about how they put tags around their necks so they wouldn't get lost, that had "Crested Butte" destination on them. And they got off at Ellis Island . . . and then they put them on the train for Crested Butte . . . They knew nothing about the country, nothing about the language, and they just got on the boat and went. You kind of wonder. Anything was better than what they left, I guess. I don't know how they did it. You know, it'd take a lot of nerve to do something like that.[1]

Joe Danni

Most of the parents of Crested Butte old-timers came from Italy and the Balkans. Eastern and southern European people began departing in the 1880s, the biggest waves leaving by the turn of the century. Like so many who emigrated, they left because they had little at home, and they saw America as the land of opportunity.[2]

Many of the Italians who came to Crested Butte were from the Piedmont area. The Slavic immigrants came from various parts of Croatia and Slovenia, the two regions that sent the greatest number of immigrants to the United States. Both were ruled by the Hapsburg Dynasty until the collapse of the Austro-Hungarian Empire in 1918, when they became two of the six republics that made up Yugoslavia.[3]

Croatians were among the first Europeans to emigrate to the Western Hemisphere as merchants, sailors, and missionaries. On the eve of the Civil War, nearly three thousand lived in the southern United States. They began to arrive in more significant numbers in the 1870s, and by 1880, at least twenty thousand Croatians lived in the United States, mostly in the West. The largest wave, about four hundred thousand, came in the years 1890 to 1917.

Elk Avenue, Crested Butte, 1880s

Most of the Slovenians who came were from the province of Carniola. There is no reliable data, but it is estimated that from 1850 to 1914, 315 thousand people left Slovenia for the United States. The greatest numbers arrived along with the Croatians during the period from 1880 to 1914.[4]

Both Slavic groups were part of what was called the "New Immigration," referring to the huge number of people that came after 1880. They were mostly peasants from rural areas in southern and eastern Europe, and they came primarily for economic reasons. Problems of overpopulation in intensely agrarian areas, due to the landholding patterns of small farms with very large families, forced younger sons to leave home in order to survive. Over eighty percent of the immigrants from these areas were unskilled or semi-skilled male workers, and they went wherever they could find employment. Large numbers of them ended up in the depressed slums of urban areas, while others settled in smaller towns in the midwestern and western United States. Many looked for work in coal mines, having been miners before or having heard about the opportunity, and one of their destinations was Crested Butte. By 1920, the town's 1,213 residents included five hundred Croatians, making

Elk Mountain House, 1880s

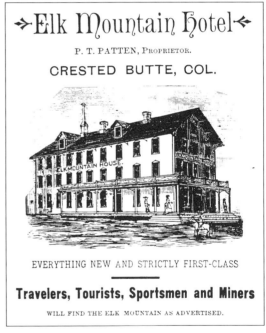

Crested Butte's Slavic population larger than that of Denver.[5]

The journey from the Old Country to Crested Butte consisted of a minimum of nine days by ship from Croatia and Slovenia to New York City, and then five days across the country by train. Many men sent back for wives and relatives after they found steady employment.[6]

Johnny Krizmanich, whose large, strong hands and swollen knuckles are testimony to the years he spent in the coal mines, says his father came in 1895 or 1897, his mother in 1902. They married in Crested Butte soon after they met. His parents, like so many others, "came to find something else, something more, because there was nothing there for them. You know, in the Old Country they had real small farms. Twenty people in the house." Because Johnny's father died when he was very young, he has only a vague account of his father's reasons for coming. According to the story, his father "had a very small family . . . Him and another brother had a small place, a ranch, nothing—a little bitty farm." The tradition of primogeniture forced his father to leave: ". . . my dad was the youngest out of two boys, so the oldest one would have got the place, and that's why my dad come to this country. How? He probably knew somebody who'd come over. At that time there was lots of them coming over."[7]

John Somrak, who also spent many years in the coal mines, remembers: "My mother said it took them fourteen days to come across the ocean. Didn't know one word of English—just hang a shipping tag on your neck and let you go. And she said it was tough on the ship and they got sick and every other darn thing." John's father came just before the turn of the century. Like other young men who came alone, he went back and forth as many as "four different times" and "finally, about the end of 1910, he decided to stay." His mother came in 1913.[8]

Guisieppo and Mary Danni with their children Anton and Katherine, c. 1897. Guisieppo, or "Joe," came to Crested Butte first, then sent for his wife and children.

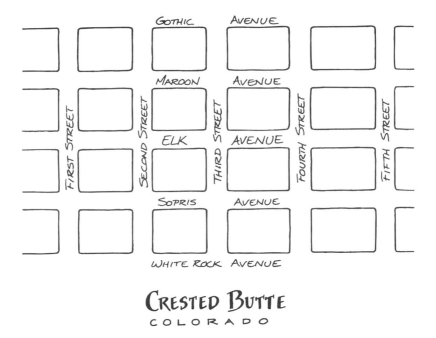

The newcomers had varied expectations. Johnny Krizmanich says his parents were content with what they found when they arrived:

> I think it was better than they expected. In the Old Country, everything was so poor and the people was so poor, and they knew there was no future for them anymore. So they thought it was pretty nice in Crested Butte. My father even used to ask my mother years later if she ever wanted to go back. She said "No—this is my home."

Others who ended up in Crested Butte, like so many of the immigrants who came to this country, had been drawn by tales of quick and easy money. People like Teeny Tezak's parents, who came from Slovenia, had such high expectations that they were destined to be disappointed with what they found:

Dad stopped in Pennsylvania. I guess he was in the coal mines there. They said that money's easier to make in Colorado. He found out it wasn't. A more rugged life, snow and everything. Long winters. I imagine life was harder than they expected. Of course I know one thing. They was told that they could pick money on trees or bushes or rocks or any place. Roll a rock on its side and I'll find money under it. When they come to this country, well they found there wasn't no money no place. Mama used to say that when she left her mother, her mother was crying, and she said, "Mama, don't cry." She says, "I'll fill this suitcase with money and I'll be right back." She never did go back.[9]

THE IMMIGRANTS

The life awaiting the immigrants when they arrived in Crested Butte was unexpectedly harsh. Long winters in the high mountain valley brought snows that accumulated up to twenty feet deep and lasted for as long as nine months of the year. Economic strains and personal tragedies were an inevitable part of life in a coal mining town. And, of course, they grappled with learning a new language and adjusting to a new culture.

Tensions arose. With the arrival of the new immigrants, Crested Butte became a town made up of multiple and competing ethnic groups. The patterns of behavior in places like New York and Chicago were replicated on a small scale, with different nationalities associating, at least on a social level, more among themselves than with those of different backgrounds. The division of the town into sections according to ethnicity, described by Joe Saya, mimicked the ethnic neighborhoods of large cities, and was a pattern that would continue into the lives of the immigrants' children: "You take Whiterock down there, it was mostly Italians. And then up on Sopris, there was mostly Yugoslavian, Slovenian. And on the other side, on Maroon, there was mostly English and Irish and different types." Rudy Sedmak says Whiterock was referred to as "Macaroni Avenue, because the Italians lived on the lower end of the street."

MINERS' HEADQUARTERS.

—THE—

Crested ✣ Butte ✣ House.

$2.00 PER DAY. $7 and $8 PER WEEK.

TABLE FIRST CLASS.

ELK AVE., NEXT TO POSTOFFICE.   J. J. PHELAN, Prop.

South side of Elk Avenue, c. 1890

Prejudice among the first settlers of British background against the new Italian and Slavic peoples prevailed in many aspects of town life, but the discrimination usually took a subtle form. Local newspaper stories, for example, portrayed the immigrants in a negative light, reporting only criminal and other offensive acts, and ignoring any positive impact the newcomers had on the town.[1] Joe Saya recalls stories about blatant prejudice experienced by the immigrants:

> There was all kinds of nationalities up there. Italians, Slovenians, Germans, and Irish and Welshmen . . . Some of them treated us the same, and some didn't. Some thought they were better. Well, I used to hear them tell, in the olden days . . . when the miner come home . . . he'd go downtown to get a beer, and for twenty five cents he'd get a bucket full of beer. And some of them people, they'd go by there and see Slovenians and they'd spit in the bucket.

Other sources of insult were the well-known pejorative nicknames: Slovenians were "round-heads," and Italians were "dagos." The name-calling went both ways, however, and "round-heads" referred to those of British background as "Jackers" and "cousin Jacks." Rudy Sedmak remembers the origin of the nickname "cousin Jack": "When the Englishmen came across from England, finally, after they got settled and had some money, they'd say, 'Hey, Mr. Boss, do you have a job for my cousin Jack?' From then on, everyone who came from England was a cousin Jack."[2]

John Somrak explains the most creative names of all, "egg eaters" and "pie-cakers":

> . . . the Englishmen and Irish, when they went to work in the mines, you could always tell what they had for breakfast. They never used to wipe their face, so they'd have egg sticking around their mouths and their lips. So the Slavs started naming them egg eaters. Then the next name we had for them was . . . See, Slovenians and Italian people never ate pie or cake—they didn't know what the hell it was, you know what I mean? But with them guys, they ate it all the time, they had pie and cake—the English people and Scottish people and Irish . . . so some of them old Slovenian old-timers from the Old Country, out mining coal they'd say, "'pie-cakers'—how the hell are they going to work on pie and cake? You need some good old sauerkraut and smoked ham and smoked beef and stuff to eat."[3]

The new immigrant population was not without its own divisions. Fred Yaklich says that there were always arguments in Crested Butte between people who were from different parts of the Balkans: "It was all the time, you know. Like, some were from some parts of Yugoslavia, and some, they'd always, even in the pool halls, they always thought they'd come from a better place than the other ones did. It was just like Gunnison and Crested Butte, at one time they were feuding all the time." Leola Yaklich remembers how the immigrant community divided during World War II: "Can you believe that during World

Office of the *Elk Mountain Pilot* Newspaper, c. 1890

War II the factions here split up—the Croatians, the Slovenes, the Serbs. Some were for Tito, and others weren't. They all began fighting this war here. It was unbelievable, you know . . . it was simply arguments." Fred adds: "This was just verbal." And the antagonism never lasted long: "Oh, there was an argument, and then the next day they'd probably be drinking beer together in the pool hall. I imagine it went that way all over the country."[4]

Most of the early prejudice was aimed at the immigrants from southern and central Europe. Despite it, they retained as many aspects of their culture as they could, continuing customs and traditions, and teaching their children their native languages. The small size of Crested Butte insured that the different ethnic groups did not completely insulate themselves from each other. Indeed, there was much sharing and overlapping of cultures.

Betty Spehar describes growing up in Crested Butte as having "the best of two worlds. So much that was marvelous from that European culture. Mr. Welch across the alley teaching us a little bit of Italian. And, you know, all of the other celebrations, too, you had the marvelous Patron of Miners, and there were some Germans and so we got into some German traditions."[5]

Fraternal lodges form a funeral procession on Elk Avenue, 1920s

The immigrants also created formal and informal systems of guidance and support which were essential aspects of their new life in Crested Butte. They established a precedent for supplying various forms of assistance to others in need which were passed along to their children. Fraternal lodges played an important role by providing the immigrants with security and a place to gather and socialize with others of the same ethnic background. With a population of less than two thousand, Crested Butte had four or five Italian and ten southern Slav societies. The first fraternal lodge, the Society of St. Joseph, was established in 1893.[6]

As Rudy Sedmak remembers, membership in the lodges was a part of everyone's lives: "First thing they'd do when you was born is put you in a lodge, for insurance purposes." Joe Saya says participation was taken very seriously:

In them days, they were pretty strict. If you didn't attend a meeting, it was a dollar fine. And when somebody passed away and there was a funeral, if you didn't attend the funeral, it was two dollars. They were all big funerals. Just about everybody in town knew each other, and when somebody passed away, they all went to the funeral. We had a parade, from town up to the cemetery. And everybody would wear their lodge badges and everything.

Unlike the indigenous American lodges such as the Masons and the Knights of Pythia, which tended to put more emphasis on secret ritual, one of the most important functions of the ethnic lodges was to provide insurance to the sick, widows, and orphans, and to fund the funeral services of their members. Fred Yaklich, whose father was very active in St. Joseph's and St. Mary's, says about the lodges: "It was a tradition, you know, burial insurance, and then they had benefits. It was more like an insurance company."7

Knights of Pythia Hall, 1960s

The lodges maintained cultural traditions with music and dances, holiday celebrations and other social functions. Betty Spehar remembers the joys of the various Croatian traditions, especially baptisms and long wedding celebrations which often included parties in the lodges:

Oh, well, there were weddings that lasted for days with dancing and musicians and things. When I was five and I was the flower girl in my cousin Mary's wedding . . . I wore this gorgeous yellow chiffon dress, and went to the celebration, and it was still going on Sunday, and you were dressed up, but differently dressed. And then on Monday, I was in my play clothes . . . and I wandered over to see my auntie, and the musicians were still playing, and people were still dancing, and food was still plentiful! So it was really lovely.[8]

Probably the best known lodge was the Society of the Blessed Virgin Mary of Perpetual Aid, or St. Mary's—commonly referred to as the Croatian Lodge. St. Mary's took over the former Knights of Pythia Hall and moved it, in 1902, from Elk Avenue down to Second Street. After opening a saloon on the bottom floor, it became a central community meeting place, much like Town Hall, and was rented out to groups on various occasions, including meetings of the Knights of Pythia and the Democratic Party, and family wedding receptions. (Today, St. Mary's is the Crested Butte Athletic Club).

Another strong force in immigrant life was the Catholic Church. St. Patrick's Church was built in the 1880s when most of the Catholics were Scottish and Irish. After 1900, its diverse congregation was made up mostly of Slavs and Italians and, in later years,

Croatian Hall, 1972

Mexicans. In the 1930s, St. Patrick's served six hundred to seven hundred Catholics of various backgrounds.⁹

Religion was the cause of the most serious forms of prejudice. John Somrak remembers ongoing tension: "You know, the Protestants and the Catholics never did get along. That was one fight that was going on up there all the time. They didn't get along until later years when everybody started mellowing a little bit and softening up and decided we should just all work together . . ." John remembers the worst years of bigotry during the 1920s when the Ku Klux Klan came to town, recruited members, and burned crosses on a hill known as Chocolate Peak just east of town. He says the KKK stood for a definition of an American that excluded people like him: "You had to be a white person, you had to be no foreigner, and you had to be Protestant."¹⁰

The Ku Klux Klan Ticket

United States Senator, to fill vacancy
RICE W. MEANS
Justice of Supreme Court
JOHN T. ADAMS
Governor
CLARENCE J. MORLEY
Lieutenant Governor
EINAR J. WALLINGER
Secretary of State
CARL S. MILLIKEN
Auditor of State
CHARLES DAVIS
State Treasurer
WM. D. MacGINNIS
Attorney General
WILLIAM LOUIS BOATRIGHT
State Supt. of Public Instruction
ELSIE ROBINS FOOTE
Regent of the University of Colorado
HENRY W. CATLIN
State Senator, First Sen. District,
(Vote for Three)
GOLDING FAIRFIELD
ALEXANDER R. YOUNG
A. E. BOGDON
20 (Over)

Klansman Clarence J. Morley won the governorship of Colorado on the Republican ticket in 1924.

Fred Yaklich also remembers the Klan as being the cause of the greatest divisions in town:

> It was in the twenties. I know they'd be burning crosses and circles up there. We used to be in school, and we used to watch them parade. Somebody'd die, and they all had their robes. Nobody would admit, you know, that they belonged to the Ku Klux Klan, but our janitor was just a little short fellow, and we always knew he was there . . . I'd

say maybe about four years they were pretty strong . . . It got to where they were firing shots . . . and then it kind of died down.

By the end of the 1920s, the influence of the Klan began to ebb. The Catholic Church remained an integral part of life in Crested Butte and the immigrants saw a gradual growth in religious tolerance.[11]

The first step in adjusting to America was learning to speak English, a challenge that was quickly met by the men when they entered the work force. The women, because they spent most of their time at home, had more difficulty learning the new language. Betty Spehar says her father catered to the wives of immigrants by having different languages spoken in his store: "The women were able to shop in their own language, which was of great comfort to them. One lady just absolutely cried when Dad understood her German, she was so relieved." Teeny Tezak's mother, like many women, never did learn how to speak English well, but his father's English speaking and writing skills were a source of pride: "Mama got to where she could understand pretty good, but she never could talk it. And Dad, you'd never say he was foreign born! Other guys told him, if he was born in the Old Country, he must've went to school here. He never did. But he could talk and write just the same as anybody else."[12]

In addition to keeping religious and cultural traditions alive, the immigrants felt strongly that their native European languages should be spoken by their children. Language was the simplest and most direct means they had of maintaining a connection with their homeland, and of passing their ethnic identity down to the second generation.

John Somrak, like so many others, grew up in a household in which only Croatian was spoken:

> Our family didn't know one word of English until I was . . . seven years old. I didn't go to school until I was seven years old—too small. My mother wouldn't send me the first year. She waited 'til my other brother was old enough so she could send two of us to school. We didn't know one word of English. Our neighbor guy took us to school, Tony Orazem, and told the teacher what our names was, and we started from there.[13]

St. Patrick's Church

Tony Mihelich also spoke Croatian growing up, and studied it in classes that were taught in St. Mary's Lodge by the first-generation immigrants: "I can still talk it and read it and write it. Of course, we went to school up there, at the Crested Butte Health Club. We used to go up there certain nights a week, maybe four, and learn our language. It

Ernestine Block and Alberta Metzler dressed for the Fourth of July. Traditionally, Elk Avenue was lined with cut spruces topped with American flags.

was mostly in the summer."14 Johnny Krizmanich's father, Steven Krizmanich taught a night school course in Croatian at the lodge from 1914 until the mid-twenties.

CF&I, meanwhile, was eager to speed the process of Americanization. The company provided some classes in English, American government, and American history. It also, however, catered to the diversity of its mining communities by publishing a weekly magazine, *Camp & Plant*, which printed articles in various languages. Established in 1904, the magazine contained reports from local mining camps on social events and articles that focused on different subjects ranging from technical aspects of coal mining to the status of local kindergartens. Much of the material was written purposefully to infuse a sense of pride among the miners in their work and the magazine contained messages to encourage diligence and ambition. Typical was the back cover of one of its issues from 1928 with this quote from Benjamin Franklin entitled "Industry":

> An hour's industry will do more to produce cheerfulness, suppress evil humours and retrieve your affairs, than a month's moaning. Sloth makes all things difficult, but industry all easy; and he that riseth late must trot all day and shall scarce overtake his business at night; while laziness travels so slowly that poverty soon overtakes him.[15]

The immigrants readily adopted American holidays and celebrations and rapidly achieved citizenship. It seems that the cultural cohesiveness and support which characterized early life in Crested Butte allowed them to become quickly Americanized. Their ability to maintain their own traditions and socialize among people of the same ethnic background gave them the security necessary to engender a sense of pride in and devotion to their new country.

The newcomers' eagerness to adapt to life as Americans was evident in their participation in government. According to Johnny Krizmanich, his parents understood and appreciated the new freedom they had in this country, and its attendant responsibilities:

> You bet my parents voted. Strictly Democrat. Franklin D. Roosevelt was next to God. That was one of their privileges, you know. In the Old

Country, they didn't have any of that. You didn't have no privilege at all. They were under this Franz Joseph, the big shot of Austria-Hungary.[16]

The patriotism of the small, heterogeneous population was further evidenced by their pride in the number of soldiers they sent to World War I, and those their children sent to World War II. Fred Yaklich remembers that Crested Butte sent eighty seven men of his generation to fight in World War II and suffered three casualties. The yearly celebration of the Fourth of July was always the most festive occasion of the year. As Joe Saya remembers:

Fourth of July was the biggest celebration. Did the same they do now, we had parades and races, we had baseball games in them days, Crested Butte would play Paonia or Somerset teams, and then the fireworks. And one thing they don't have now we used to have every morning was sunrise, daybreak, they'd set off dynamite blasts. About four o'clock you could hear the blasts. Whoever wants to walked in the parades. In them days . . . different lodges . . . used to have their uniform and all that, and they all used to parade.[17]

The children of the immigrants benefited from their parents' swift adaptation to American life, as well as from the traditions that were maintained, the support systems that were established, and the overall community that their parents struggled to build.

Fire Department Hose Team, Fourth of July, 1896

Foot race on Elk Avenue, Fourth of July, early 1900s

One of the crucial advantages members of the second generation had over their parents in adjusting to American society was that they learned English at an early age. Rudy Sedmak, who was one of Steve Krizmanich's students, says he never did learn to speak his parents' native language very well because the emphasis was always on learning English. Even if they spoke their mother tongue at home, children quickly learned English on the streets and at school. Matt Malensek recognizes how important this was in adapting to life in Crested Butte; according to his observations, the ability of children to speak English resulted in less ethnic differentiation among the second generation: "Of course, English was the main thing. Everybody had to know that. There was more prejudice when they came, but the first thing kids'd do, we'd get acquainted. They didn't mind us kids playing. They thought that was okay."[18]

Lodges were not as important to the children of the immigrants because they did not need the social and financial guidance that was so essential for their parents. Johnny Krizmanich explains the different needs of the first and second generations:

> The idea when they first built those lodges was to keep all the people more or less together; you know, to remember the Old Country. And the insurance policies. I think the maximum you could get if somebody died was $700, $800. My generation didn't spend much time in the lodges. After my dad died, we pretty much dropped out.

Rudy Sedmak adds that later on the lodges ceased being places that separated people of different ethnic backgrounds from each other: "After a while, all the nationalities were taken in. Everyone went everywhere. There was Italian people in the Croatian Hall . . ."[19]

Many European customs continued in Crested Butte, including the preparation of ethnic foods, the music, polkas, wedding receptions and funeral services, and of course various Catholic traditions. Those customs that continued, however, were usually ones that were shared with the entire community rather than being limited to a single group of a particular ethnic background. Despite their awareness of their ethnic roots, second-generation immigrants were Americans from birth, and their identity was rooted in that experience.

THE WORK

While strong cultural traditions and celebrations were an integral part of the Crested Butte community, it was coal mining that dominated people's lives. The mines drew the immigrants to Crested Butte to begin with, and the second generation continued to work in them and assumed their children would do the same. For most of the first- and second-generation immigrants, coal mining was the only way of life they knew. It shaped their basic pattern of existence, and the unpredictable nature of the work directly or indirectly affected the lives of everyone in the town. In the end, while mining was an occupation that could be characterized by competition, it also gave common experience to people who together participated in labor struggles, survived long periods of unemployment, and consistently endured daily hardships.

Mine-related work started as early as the age of eight or nine for children who "picked slate," which consisted of removing impure pieces of rock from the coal as it came out of the mine. According to Fred Yaklich, some children at that age entered the mines with their fathers: "There was fellas up here that started when they were nine years old. There was no laws in those days. A lot of kids would just go in the mines, you know, to help their dad. But they wouldn't get paid anything. Just to help." Yaklich himself started in the

Building the tipple of the Big Mine, c. 1893–1894. The tipple is the structure from which the coal cars are tipped over to pour the coal into railroad cars.

Peanut Mine when he was sixteen. Most young men began to work officially when they were seventeen or eighteen since there was a supposed minimum age of eighteen.[1]

Rudy Sedmak, who began working at sixteen in the Horace Anthracite—later called the Peanut Mine—says the new miners were often paired up with older partners: "Usually they put a younger miner with an older miner. I worked with Frank Slogar for about ten years. They called him 'I loves to work,' but we got along. I got with him, and stayed with him until the mine shut down. He took care of me."[2]

Teeny Tezak remembers adjusting to his new surroundings in the mine when he first went to work at age seventeen:

The Big Mine, c. 1896, south side of Crested Butte. Railroad cars on tracks parallel to White Rock Avenue wait to pick up coal from the tipple at the end of Second Avenue. The smoke in the background is from burning coke ovens.

It wasn't bad once you got used to it. At first, it was kind of scary. Different than being outside. All you had was that light . . . on your forehead . . . You couldn't see nothing. Had some carbide lamps, they wasn't as good and they wasn't as safe as the electric lamps that come out afterwards, battery type. In the Big Mine, it was six thousand feet to the inside parting (where the railroad track split into two sections so that incoming and outgoing cars could pass each other). So let's see, I'd go in about eight thousand feet. I mostly drove mules. Pulling coal from the loaders, and loading coal. You give an empty tin to two men within, and pull the loaded coal out and then give a tin to two others and pull their load out, give them an empty tin and then come back . . .[3]

The process of extracting the coal began, according to Fred Yaklich, with blasting, followed by shovelling and loading the carts:

Horace Anthracite, later the Peanut Mine, looking up the Slate River Valley

The shot setters were the fire bosses. You'd drill your holes in, put your caps and powder at night in the mine, in your room, and then the fire boss'd come and set them off when there was no one in the mine. And then he'd check for methane, too. In the smaller mines, you'd do your own thing. When you got through working for the day, you'd drill your holes, put your powder in there, and three o'clock come, everybody had to get out. So you'd maybe have forty, fifty feet of fuse . . . because they'd run about a minute a foot, so you had a lot of time, and you'd shoot your own shots . . . We each had our own room. You might have somebody maybe twenty, thirty feet away from you in another room . . . Your coal, if you drilled good and got a good shot in, you'd have coal to shovel all day. If you got the carts. They had what they called "trips." There were usually sixteen carts to a trip. They'd pull them out of each entry and haul them out to the tipple and dump them in the railroad cars.[4]

Rudy Sedmak, who worked for CF&I for twenty six years, explains the way the carts worked:

Lunchtime at the Forest Queen Mine, Irwin, 1885

There was a tail rope to hold them back, to keep them from going too fast. And the head rope would pull the carts out. Outside of the mine, the engine house—the outside hoist—pulled out the "trip" of sixteen carts. There were what you call partings, two tracks. On one were the empty carts, the other had the loaded carts. The mule driver would take an empty cart, go into a room and load it with coal. He'd tend to eight or ten other people and when he got sixteen carts, he went to the main parting on the main line.[5]

The nature of the coal mining depended in part upon the size of the mine, as Fred goes on to explain:

The Big Mine was a very big mine. Some places, they probably went three, four miles in. But the Peanut Mine, you only went in probably half a mile. Maybe you'd walk it in fifteen, twenty minutes. It was a big entry, and then they had rooms branching off. When I went to the Peanut, I brought this new shovel and pick, and the Boss, the first thing he'd done was cut the handles off them 'cause the coal was only that high and you had to work in there . . . The entry was high enough for the mule to get in to pull the cart. But, see, the vein of coal was, only oh, maybe from eighteen to twenty, twenty two inches high.[6]

Joe Sedmak, like most old-timers, worked all sorts of jobs inside the mines. Whatever the job was, it always involved hard labor that did not pay well:

I tell you it was tough for $4.40 a day for about ten hours. And if you took a contract loading coal, they paid you forty seven cents a ton, that's all. And you couldn't load too many carts. I worked hard twenty years straight before they shut down. I loaded coal with my father for years, and then I was a rope rider, and then I was a mule driver, and I used to take empty carts in and have them load it and pull it out. You go underground about six or seven miles, you don't know if you're going to come out or not. Well, in the wintertime you go in when it's dark and come out when it's dark.[7]

It was demanding labor that allowed little or no time for rest, says Fred: "You'd go in the morning and stay in there 'til it was quitting time.

Cutting timber to support mining tunnels

Hauling mining timber on Elk Avenue. Ranchers bringing logs to the mines were paid in scrip which could only be spent in the company store.

Sometimes you'd eat just on the fly, take a bite when you can. If you were getting carts pretty good and you were waiting a minute, maybe you'd eat a sandwich. And if a cart came, you dropped it and loaded it and then when it'd gone if you had some time, then you'd eat another one. You just nibbled all day long at it."[8]

Johnny Krizmanich describes how he, like so many others, was hardened to the work: "You know how most kids are when they're that age, they don't care to work, do they? I did . . . I was sharpened the day I got there." What he "sharpened to" were the long hours, tedium, danger, and low wages that were all aspects of the job:

You were paid by just how much haul you load. It was starvation wages. When I first went to work there, they were paying forty seven cents a ton. You were paid by the amount of coal you could load to be shipped out. You dumped the coal out, loaded it, put oil on the track . . . You kept that up all day long . . . You had to take a brass number, a tag, and you put it on your person someplace . . . with your payroll number stamped on it. That was in case they had a big accident and you got bunged so bad that they couldn't recognize you when you was dead, you know. That would be your brass identification.

Rudy Sedmak says the brass check also enabled the company to keep track of the miners: "Every miner was given a brass check every time he went in the mine, and if that brass check wasn't back at night, they'd go in there after him. You'd hang it on your belt." The other check the miners used was the coal check, as Rudy explains: "They were about the size of a dollar — big, black checks. Before you started to work, you'd hang it up on the car. When you brought the coal out, they'd take that check off, and you'd get credit for the car full of coal."9

Yaklich recalls the amount of work all the contract miners had to do for which they were not rewarded: "It was all

Brass life check — miners climbed steps up the hill to "the shed," entered the bathhouse to change into work clothes, and went to the lamproom to pick up a lamp and a life check — about the size of a half dollar. A life check missing from the board at the end of the day indicated an accident had occurred.

contract work. There was so much dead work you done that you never got paid for. You'd go in there and work all day long, maybe, and all dead work and never make a nickel."[10]

Accidents in the mines were a part of everyday life. The worst accident in Crested Butte history, and one of the worst in all of Colorado mining, was the Jokerville Mine explosion in 1884 in which sixty miners were killed. All of the miners were of English origin, evidence of a period of unusual ethnic homogeneity in the history of the town. After the disaster at the Jokerville, the accident rate in Crested Butte improved — from 1916 to 1929, five men were killed in the Big Mine, and ten were killed in the other three CF&I-operated mines.[11]

In addition to the mine-related deaths, however, there were huge numbers of injuries. John

Somrak points out that this danger was an inevitable part of the job: "There was accidents of all sorts. Any time you're going under a mountain with all that bad roof and rock above you and then gas— I mean foul air—you're fighting all the odds."[12]

Teeny Tezak sustained a number of injuries:

> First I had a leg broke, in three places, below the knee. I was back to work, but doing light work. And then in '42 I had a skull fracture. I was a trip rider, is what they're called, and the trip had started down this steep grade. A timber fell out and banged against the car and ended up jumping. It must have hit the rail and then my head. Anyways, they said be grateful, my head was inside and the hard hat was smashed. Probably would have crushed my head. I was off quite a while, I don't remember just how long. And they put me on light work again.[13]

Before the unions came in, the miners had no power to improve their working conditions. CF&I dominated Crested Butte mining, and was for the most part callous to the hardships of its workers. It wielded tremendous power all over Colorado, creating a base for economic growth by drawing capital and labor and encouraging other forms of development related to manufacturing and transportation.[14] By 1903, ten percent of all Colorado wage earners depended on the company and it was the most important in the state.

The CF&I Colorado Supply Store

Since coal was usually discovered in isolated areas, companies such as CF&I built many company towns to attract workers and their families. Given the remoteness of these communities, the residents had no choice but to depend on the company for educational, medical, and social services as well as for housing. Living in rugged country and working under harsh and dangerous conditions for an uncaring and sometimes neglectful employer created the physical and cultural deprivation that marked so many company towns at the turn of the century.[15]

Fortunately, although it was the largest of CF&I's mountain operations in the early 1900s, Crested Butte never fit entirely into the category of company town. It existed before any of the company mines were opened, and much of its property and business was privately owned. The only property in town owned by the company was the Big Mine, the superintendent's house up on Big Mine Hill, a lodge for single miners, the Colorado Supply Store, and a group of houses for employees called "New Town." Nor was CF&I the dominant influence socially and culturally, due to the strong traditions and ties in Crested Butte's small community. Finally, the company was not the only employer. In the lives of the old-timers, there were five other

Housing built by CF&I then called "New Town." One block stands today on Gothic between 1st and 2nd Streets. The remaining houses were moved to Gunnison in the 1950s.

Mules hauling coal carts inside a tunnel

mines in Crested Butte: the Buckley, Pueblo, Pershing, Smith Hill, and Peanut. Moreover, some citizens had their own businesses, including competing stores which ensured that the Company Supply Store did not have a monopoly.[16]

Most Crested Butte residents nevertheless relied on the company for their livelihood because the majority of the men worked at the Big Mine. CF&I blew whistles

Coal mine entry

throughout town to announce the daily mining schedule. John Somrak recalls that everyone depended on the whistle not just for the announcement of their daily routine, but also for notice of unemployment and hard times to come due to the inconsistency of work which plagued the industry:

> In the morning, when the mine would work, they'd blow the whistle at five in the morning at the mine, to wake up the miners. At 6:00 they'd blow two blasts—it's time to leave home and go for the mine. Seven o'clock they'd blow one blast—that was starting time. And if you went underground you had to get there earlier. Then at 11:30 or 12:00 they used to blow it—noontime—everybody in town used to go by that. It was lunchtime . . . after a half hour, it was over with. Then at 4:30 in the afternoon was supposed to be quitting time—like I told you, nine-hour days—that was the end of the day. Then at 5:00 they'd blow it again and that was the signal if there's going to be work the next day or not, and one long whistle was work tomorrow—two short ones, no work. That's what we used to go by. In the wintertime, most of the time it was one whistle, because you'd work steady, five days a week, six days a week. Summertime there wasn't much. Spring every year they'd slack up, too, there'd be one day, two days, three days a week, nothing.[17]

The Big Mine with Gothic and Snodgrass Mountains in the background. Coal was burned in six furnaces, known as "boilers," which heated water to furnish electricity to the mine and the company houses on the hill. The boilers are located in the building on the right. The long snowshed covered the tramway which carried coal cars from the engine room at the mouth of the mine to the tipple where the coal was sorted by grade and dumped into waiting railroad cars.

If the whistle blew when it was not scheduled to, it meant that an accident had occurred. As Fred Yaklich recalls: "They used to have a whistle blow when somebody got killed. They'd just keep a-blowing that whistle." Leola Yaklich remembers the fear that would suddenly strike the town: "If a whistle blew in the middle of the day when it wasn't supposed to, you knew it was a mine accident. And then all the women in town tied their little babushkas on and went to the mine. It was then the women had that terrible fear, you know, not knowing if it was their man, or someone in their family. And the kids, everybody just ran for that mine entrance."¹⁸

There was less mining in the summertime because warm weather caused a decline in the demand for fuel. The lack of steady work forced many miners to search for other jobs in the summer months, and to hunt and fish when there was no money to buy food. Everybody did a lot of hunting and fishing, says Tony Mihelich, "because in those days that's what you survived on."¹⁹

Teeny Tezak used to work on the Malensek ranch and other ranches in the area during the summer months, and he also managed to find year-round weekend work with a local freight company that brought groceries, mail, and other goods to places like Gothic and Smith Hill. Many women also planted private gardens during the short three-month growing season which supplied the family with some fresh vegetables.

Mining was an irregular means of employment, characterized by hardship and struggle. But like the ethnic conflicts, conditions in the mines gradually improved. Johnny Krizmanich says about the CF&I of his time: "Oh, I don't think it was any different from any other mining company. They were all pretty much the same. They made it pretty rough until the unions got in. Then the unions told them they had to change their ways."²⁰

All the old-timers agree that before the United Mine Workers of America (UMW) signed a contract with CF&I in 1933, the company was, in the words of Johnny, "terrible—in every way." There is evidence that the company controlled local elections, and it paid its miners in scrip up until 1914, which could only be used to buy goods at the Company Store, usually at inflated prices. Ruthless exploitation, particularly of the immigrants, was typical in the coal mines; mules were generally worth more to CF&I than men, and many miners lost their lives working in gaseous, unsafe mines. The newest immigrants were typically given the least desirable, most dangerous jobs and received the lowest wages.[21]

Mule yard on Big Mine Hill, now called "the bench," with the superintendent's house and Mt. Emmons in the background.

Some of the jobs in the mine were definitely better than others, as Johnny Krizmanich explains: "Well, the bosses was one category. And the guys that was cutting coal, they made more money. And a lot of guys that were just hand loading it made a lot. But then the rest of them made the same." The bosses, as Fred Yaklich explains, were those responsible for giving orders and keeping an eye on the other miners: "The bosses went around to see that you were doing your work, they'd check who goes to work, how much coal you'd load . . . and they could fire you if they wanted to."[22]

Before the union came in full force, it was usually those of British background who got the more desirable jobs. The supervisor and most of the mine bosses — the workers responsible for giving orders — were of British origin, and Krizmanich says they tended to favor others of the same background: "As a rule, you could figure that the English-speaking one was gonna stick to the English people." Fred adds: ". . . sure there were a lot of times where you wouldn't see eye to eye with the bosses. They wanted to get everything they could out of you. They just kept pushing you."23

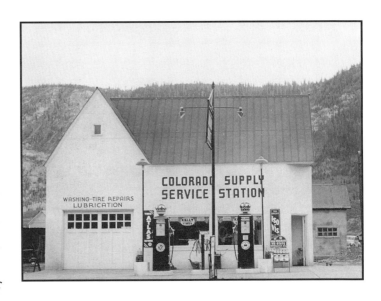

Run by CF&I, the Colorado Supply service station was across Elk Avenue from the Colorado Supply Store.

Bribery was a common practice in the mines, as Fred remembers: "If you could butter the boss up, you might get an extra cart, a little better room, something like that." Krizmanich adds: "When I first went to work in the mine, a lot of these people, they would kick back some of their wages to the boss so they would get a job that they could make more money on it." But Krizmanich was one of the miners who learned to rely instead on his own hard work: ". . . I didn't go along with that. I figured what little I was getting, I earned. I'm not gonna give it to the boss."24

The immigrants and their children learned early on that the only honest means of getting a better job was to prove themselves to the bosses through hard labor. Many old-timers agree that the immigrant miners worked harder. As Teeny Tezak says: "[The Slovenians and the Croatians] was money hungry . . . That way they'd have a better life and have more to save. They started with less. At first, they didn't care how they was treated just as long as they had a job. To make a dollar or two."25

John Somrak says his own persistent hard work sprang from the need his parents felt to raise themselves from a position of disadvantage:

> We had what they call the bottom line and I mean you had to work up that line. But we proved ourselves, too. Because the Slavs and the Croatians, they were god-darned good workers. It's just the nature of our people, they were born that way. In other words, they're bred that way. Hard working. Back in the foreign countries, that's all there was, hard work, and that's the only way you could live, or get going, or make something of yourself . . . The only way you could get up there was you got to prove yourself, and buck the god-darned line, which we did—I did. A lot of guys wouldn't do it, they just stayed where they were. I said to hell with staying there. I'm going to buck it. And I did.[26]

The first- and second-generation immigrants might have initially been willing to work harder and for lower wages than their English co-workers in order to better their situation, but they, too, wanted greater reward for their work and began to turn to organized labor as a means of improving the quality of their jobs. CF&I had gradually made changes in the early 1900s in response to growing labor agitation. In 1901, the company established its Sociological Department to address conditions in the coal towns, which until then the company had largely ignored. In many of the towns, CF&I was the only employer, only landowner, and the dominant influence in people's lives. Although this was not the case in Crested Butte, the company was still influential, particularly with its programs concerning immigrant workers. The Department's declared goals were, among other things, to support kindergartens, aid public schools, help to establish reading rooms and night schools, improve employee housing, and provide circulating libraries and art collections.[27]

Rudy Sedmak remembers some of the CF&I programs that were a compulsory part of community life:

They had a Home Safety chapter of CF&I. All the miners were asked to be there—you didn't have much choice. They put on a program, and all the families went. They had a great time, down at the school gymnasium. The school kids would put on a play, a little skit, or someone would read some poetry. A little bit of entertainment. There were a few refreshments, and talks on safety, or awards.[28]

Despite the company's efforts to appease its workers, labor unrest continued and worsened. Miners in Crested Butte and the neighboring settlement of Floresta went on strike in October of 1913 and both the Big Mine and the Floresta Mine closed. Perhaps because the community of Crested Butte was not completely owned and controlled by the company, the town escaped violence,[29] but Joe Saya remembers the scabs (men willing to do the work of the miners on strike) and armed men that were brought in: "Militia came to Crested Butte to protect the scabbing because of the union men. They'd figured there'd be trouble. They were dressed up just like the state patrol are now, with those hats, and their uniforms. They were parading around the streets . . ."[30] The strike continued until November 1914, over a year after it had begun.

The strikes in Crested Butte caused new animosity in the town. Fred Yaklich explains that some of the miners supported the unionization efforts, while others did not: "There were scabs, you know, and they'd go to work.

And some didn't work so it started a lot of feuds." Leola Yaklich adds that while some miners continued to work to support their families, "The strikes instigated a lot of feuds because for some, it was imperative that they work or their children starved. And the others resented that they scabbed. And it was never forgotten."[31]

Families in the Ludlow tent colony, April 1914

Meanwhile, serious violence was occurring elsewhere. One of the most infamous events in labor history was the "Ludlow Massacre" which took place in the southern part of the state. During the winter of 1913–1914, coal miners, backed by the United Mine Workers of Colorado (UMW), went on strike all over Colorado. In Las Animas County, not far from Crested Butte, the management of CF&I closed its mines and forced families out of company housing. Workers and their families moved into tent camps, one of which was built on a railroad siding known as Ludlow. In April 1924, gunfire broke out between the strikers and the gunmen brought in to protect company property. The National Guard set fire to the colony and, in the end, nineteen people died, including thirteen women and children. The incident incited further violence across the state that continued until the state militia was replaced by U.S. Army troops.

Violence ceased but unrest was widespread. The next major strike in Crested Butte began in November 1927. It was supported by the Industrial Workers of the World, referred to as the "Wobblies," and went on until June of the following year. None of these early strikes resulted in satisfaction for the workers.[32] The first concession was granted in 1915 in response to the Ludlow Massacre, when CF&I initiated the Rockefeller Plan promising fair treatment of employees. It wasn't until 1933, after years of disputes, that the company finally signed a contract with the UMW meeting demands of President Roosevelt's national programs and temporarily putting an end to labor agitation. John Somrak says that the interests of the miners were always opposed to the interests of the company and that there was "no relation" between the two groups:

> . . . white and black, you know what I mean? Miners, we were there to get what we deserved, and have safe and healthy jobs, even if they were hard. And the companies were there to make money. . . . The cheaper they could get by with it, the cheaper the wages they could pay, the more work they could squeeze out of you, that's what they would do.[33]

Joe Saya agrees that the miners and the company had opposing views on how the mine should be operated. He plainly states, "I don't think CF&I was a good company . . . They wanted you to work all the time—eight, nine, ten hours—and they weren't going to pay you nothing."[34]

Not many Crested Butte old-timers who are alive today worked in the mines before the union came in. Matt Malensek was an exception. His father-in-law was renowned for his early involvement with unionization, as

After the fire, Ludlow

his sister-in-law Margaret tells: "My father was a big union man. Then they crucified him. I remember my dad used to go over the hills (walked to other towns to get work) because they called him an agitator . . . during that Ludlow thing, 1913, 1914. He was a union man even at that time."[35]

Matt, too, was an early fighter for workers' rights. One of the major issues was the very dangerous conditions in the mines, with their insufficient work space and carelessly constructed roof supports. Also controversial were the amount the miners were paid and what they were paid for, since the system of rewarding them only for the amount of coal they brought to the surface encouraged hasty, careless work underground. Matt describes the ongoing tension between unions and the company because of their disagreement over these crucial issues:

Shoes of striker's children from Ludlow

The company didn't like the unions, and the unions didn't like the company. The unions, they was trying to do for the better of humanity. I was a union man all the time. That was my big downfall, because they didn't like union men.... I joined the union in 1918. United Mine Workers. That was the whole works, the UMW. Then they got the Wobblies in there at one time and they wanted to start some other union, but the principles of the unions was different. Different kind of work and different ideas. UMW was a good union, more or less.... I was in trouble all the time, wanting different things that other people didn't care about. What the company didn't like, they didn't want to see you all the time trying to have everybody belong to the union, and trying to better conditions. The company didn't like anybody that belonged to the union.... In the mines it'd all depend on what kind of a miner you was. If you was a better miner, you'd get along better. If you was a man that understood mining quite a bit, they thought that was a good thing. But if you wasn't a good miner, why they didn't care. There were a lot more accidents, and they didn't care much about anybody getting hurt or getting killed. That didn't matter, especially if you belonged to the union.[36]

Fred Yaklich explains how early union activists were punished by the company: "They'd give you the worst place in the mine where nobody'd want to work. But if you wanted a job, you'd go third level. That was it. It was bad working, water and low coal and, you know, you just couldn't make a living out of it.... Then you knew you weren't in with the boss. Most of the time if you ever got there, you'd quit."37

According to Johnny Krizmanich, the situation of the miners started to improve significantly around the time of World War II. After CF&I signed a contract with UMW, the company eventually could no longer ignore fighters like Matt. The first noticeable improvement, says Johnny, was in the conditions of the mine, since the company was now forced to listen to what the workers had to say: "... after the union came in, you could refuse to work under those same conditions. Before, they tell you if you don't want to work, then go—we don't need you. If they try to pull that on you, you just go to the union, the committee, go see the big shots and that was it. They'd iron that out." The wages also gradually improved. Overall, according to Johnny, UMW, which all the miners had to belong to, made mining a more humane, equitable industry:

> It was a lot nicer for the people. You always felt like somebody's beating on your back before that, but after it was a lot better. The union was automatic. It was what you called "closed shop." You had to belong to the union. And you were stupid if you wouldn't, 'cause that's what put the bread and butter on the table was the union. Actually,

the miners weren't much better than slaves in those days before the unions came in.[38]

Unionization also meant that there was more equal opportunity for first- and second-generation immigrant miners to get better jobs. Once accepted, the levelling process of unionization helped to change people's attitudes, as Teeny Tezak points out: "After unionizing, they had prejudice against the guys that didn't believe much in unionization and wouldn't hardly do anything. Them's the guys there was prejudice against." John Somrak agrees that UMW made mining more fair for people like him: "There wasn't no prejudice then. It was qualifications then."[39]

After the unions were officially recognized by CF&I, the miners were treated more fairly, but mining remained a physically taxing and dangerous job. Not all Crested Butte old-timers feel the same way about their mining days. Josephine Stajduhar's husband, Reny, claimed that he would go back in the mines today if he could because, as he said, "That's all I know." Johnny Krizmanich feels strongly that mining was a way of life that perhaps only miners can truly understand and appreciate: "Well, it's hard to explain. You'd have to more or less work in it to know it. It was just awful hard labor—but it was good labor. In later years, it was good honest labor. It's what separated the men from the boys. I liked it later on."[40]

When he quit his last mining job over in Somerset in 1972, Johnny said it was because "John (his son and only child) and June both told me I worked in the mines too long." When asked if he wanted to quit, he responded, "Not really. They said after thirty five years, that was enough mining. I don't remember what I said, but I know that's the only job I ever regretted leaving. Nice people over there. Hard working. Common people. I just liked it."[41]

Joe Saya, on the other hand, says he mined only because there was no other form of employment, but he never liked it:

Well, like I say, if you're a coal miner you got a forty four jumper and a twelve shoe, and nothing in the head. All you do is pick and shovel and beat your brains out to get the coal. That means you're a big husky man, with a big jumper, a big shoe, and nothing in the head. We had to like it. We didn't have nothing else to do. It's the only way to make a living. That's all that was there. We didn't know anything else. I don't think nobody liked mining. 'Cause that was dangerous work.[42]

Most of the men in Crested Butte, as Saya points out, had no choice but to work in the mines. Coal mining provided the dominant payroll and CF&I employed most of the miners—at least 200 in the mid-1930s—in its Big Mine.[43]

Since Crested Butte was never entirely a company town, there were other forms of occupation. Tony Mihelich, for example, worked as a delivery boy for Fisher's Grocery, and then worked in the freight business and for the town before going to work for Crested Butte Hardware and Auto Supply. He considers himself lucky: "I had other jobs which were much safer and easier than the work in the mines. Because that was hazardous work. But most people worked in the mines, because that's all there was in them days. They either worked on the section of the railroad, or in the mines."[44]

Fred Yaklich's father worked thirty five years in the coal mines, but always had other work, including his dairy, which allowed him to supply milk to the small mining community of Smith Hill, located just a few miles north of town: "My dad'd ride a cow up there, milk the cow, and peddle the milk up there." Fred, who spent all of his early years mining coal, quit to take over his father's dairy business after he lost a friend in the mines following the war: "I worked in there until I went in the Navy, and then I came back, and I went back in the Big Mine, and one of my buddies there had a big slab of rock fall down and killed him, so I says 'That's it.' I walked out."45

There were also stores that competed with CF&I's Supply Store and prevented the company from having a complete monopoly over the town. Some of them were Spehar's, Verzuh's, Stefanic's, Fisher's, and Perko's. The fact that most of the names are Croatian and Slovenian shows that the immigrants were not restricted to certain types of labor and became some of Crested Butte's most successful business entrepreneurs.

Tony Stefanic explains how he got involved in the grocery business instead of working in the mines like his father:

> I was too young when I started working. Only fourteen years old. I had to be eighteen before I could work in the mines. So the guy I worked for said stick around the grocery game, so that's what I did. I had my first grocery store when I was twenty four years old. First one I bought. It was over on Grubstake, a side street. I had that for four years. Then I went up the street here to another grocery store, also my own. I was

Verzuh's Store

making good money, more than the coal miners driving mules. But if you was loading coal, you could do better.[46]

During the Depression, after the Crested Butte bank closed in 1930, the stores were essentially the bankers for everybody in town. As Eleanor Stefanic explains: "The miners were paid in checks and when they come in to pay their bills, they would sign the checks over to us and we'd deal with the banks. We had to do all the banking in Gunnison."[47]

The people who ran the groceries were in some ways better off than the miners, if only because their jobs did not entail the same dangers. Many people believe they were also better off financially. Margaret Malensek says about the store owners, "They were the people who had the money, you know. And

Joe Block's meat market

then they could loan the miners the money, too." Josephine Stajduhar agrees that those families were slightly better off, but says no one ever had much more than anyone else: "... of course they had better clothes and everything else ... but otherwise, kid, it was the same."[48]

Although the store owners had some financial advantages, unlike the miners they also had to have their own private health care and provide their own pensions. As Tony Stefanic says, "The only union I know is my own union ... You know who's going to give us a pension? We're going to make our own. Nobody else is. We had to have everything private—health care, insurance...."[49]

There is no doubt that in later years, during the time when Stefanic's was the only grocery store in town, they operated a lucrative business. But the Stefanics worked relentlessly, just as the miners did, and they endured hardships with everyone else. Tony Stefanic's story of growing up differs little from the stories of Johnny Krizmanich and Teeny Tezak:

> My folks didn't have any money. I lost my dad when I was twelve years old. He was a miner. A rock fell on his kidney, wrecked his kidney. We were on our own. We borrowed money, and we made it. Miners, they worked hard for what they got out of it, and then when we were growing up, working in the stores and all that, we had to work hard too.[50]

THE LIFE

The immigrants brought with them the tradition of having many children. Most of the families lived in crowded conditions in small, poorly insulated, box-like houses. Each house had at least one coal-burning stove that was used eight to nine months out of the year and in every backyard there stood a barn, an outhouse, a coal shed, and usually a smoke house.

While most of the men spent long days underground in the mines, the women worked to keep their houses in order, feeding the stoves, cooking for their large families, and continuously wiping, shaking, and washing away the coal dust. Doing the laundry entailed rigorous scrubbing by hand, hanging it out on the line to dry, and ironing.

Tony Mihelich recalls the endless hard work that the women did: "In them days, they done everything by hand. They would cook, sew, a lot of them even had boarders, and so they had to cook for them and do their laundry too. And a lot of them would scrub the floors on their hands and knees every day."[1] Leola and Fred Yaklich remember that the older women had a pattern to their week, and did chores together on certain days. As Fred recalls, "They had kind of a system. Mondays or Tuesdays, it was wash day. And then one day it was patching—patching clothes—and one day it was scrubbing floors and all that. And then a lot of them had hogs, you know,

A family in front of the old Slogar Bar, 1890s

and they'd cook their garbage for the hogs. And butcher the hog. They had smoke houses and they'd smoke their meat. And render all that lard from the fat." Leola adds that the pattern to women's household tasks also existed where she grew up: "I'm not a native here, but this was the same in my family. My mother washed Monday, on the board, heated water in the boiler. Tuesdays she ironed and usually baked bread, and I remember I always had to come home from school and wash those icky, sticky bread dishes. So I guess that's just the way it worked in those days."[2]

Having many babies ensured the presence of helping hands to keep the households running. It also provided better odds that some children would

Graves of children lost

survive the epidemics of diphtheria and scarlet fever that raged throughout the early decades of the 1900s. Most of the old-timers used the medical care provided by CF&I doctors, but midwives were common during that era and played a crucial role in the early days of Crested Butte.

Gwen Danni's great aunt, Annie Guilliford, aided in the births of many babies and was always there during the bleakest periods of epidemics and death. According to Gwen, Annie was also able to tell fortunes by reading tea leaves but eventually gave it up because she did not want to have to tell people about terrible times to come: "... finally she said there was too many sad things in them. Something happened that was real sad and she said she knew it was going to happen ... so she would never do it again. She said there are too many sad things to tell people and so she stopped." Gwen says about the midwives in general, "... they were just good people, that's all. Always helping somebody."[3]

A woman's burdens were greatly increased by the untimely death of her husband. In addition to the daily chores of running the household, widows would have to work in order to support their children. Joe Saya remembers the hard life his mother led after his father died:

> Maybe the hardest times was . . . when my mother had to wash clothes until we grew up and started working, all of us brothers, and then it was better. My dad died pretty young; he died when he was thirty seven years old. I was only ten years old. He died of infection. He was working in the mine and he stepped on a nail in 1915 on New Year's Eve, and gangrene set in. We buried him three weeks before my youngest brother was born. There was eight of us, five brothers and three sisters. My mother had to wash clothes to make a living. And in them days there wasn't no washing machines or anything. It was everything by hand and a scrubbing board. . . . She'd hang them out on the clothes line at night and sometimes the wind'd blow in the winter months and it'd blow the clothes off the lines and we had to go around looking for the clothes and bring them in the house so they'd dry out. They say them was the good old days. I say the good old terrible days![4]

Saya describes a past that was characterized by daily drudgery. John Somrak, who was also only a boy when he lost his father, has a similar story

Jacob "Jake" Saya c. 1914 several years before his death

The Saya family: Ann, John, Joe, Rudy, Matt, Katherine, Frank, and Jake (daughter Maria died of Scarlet fever before this photograph was taken)

to tell. He remembers the day he was told of his father's death and describes how his mother dealt with the added responsibilities with which she was suddenly faced:

> I was at school. It was up at the Big Mine — CF&I coal mine—the last one to close in Crested Butte. It was November the ninth, 1923. They were timbering up next to the roof sixteen foot high, then he slipped, fell and broke his neck. That's all there was to it—left five kids. All us boys and my sister, and she was only a year-and-a-half old, so you figure my mother had to do it from there on. She was a professional seamstress from Europe, and I mean she was professional. She could sew some of the prettiest and the best. . . . Wedding

gowns, bridesmaids' dresses, maid of honor, whatever you wanted—satin and stuff and she could make shirts and pants . . . that's how she sort of made an equal living for us guys . . . all the weddings up in Crested Butte for years she used to make all the gowns—beautiful, veils and all.[5]

Each child that survived infancy was expected to play an integral part in maintaining the household. Children were required to do all sorts of chores, from cleaning to making sure the house was provided with wood and coal to last the long, cold winters. Many left school at an early age to go out and find work to help support the family. This was mandatory in the cases where the father died early, almost always due to mine-related accidents.

Talking of their childhoods reminds the old-timers of hard work, but also of times of fun and happiness. The tasks were an accepted part of everyday life, taking time away from play, but also forcing families into cooperation and togetherness.

Margaret Malensek grew up in a family of nine children, three of whom died when they were young. She describes the crowded house in which she and her brothers and sisters grew up: "All the kids were piled up upstairs. Sometimes there was three kids on a bed. Because where there was nine of them, that took three beds!" Margaret goes on to talk about the habitual household chores, which made for a life of regularity, simplicity, and toil:

Growing up in Crested Butte, there wasn't much to it! We'd get up in the morning, work. And then after about six o'clock, we'd have our supper. But during the daytime, we always had chores to do, go to school, everything, of course. And then after you'd come home, I know after my brother passed away, the chores were mine. I had ashes to take out, I had coal to bring in. Since you had three, four stoves, you had quite a bit of ashes. In Crested Butte, we had three stoves in our house. We had one in almost every room! And if there wasn't anything else, we'd go in a little wagon and get some wood, up to Buckley or some place. In the hills there, we'd go and pick wood. So we never had no time for play. And then about six o'clock, when we did have some time to play, then we'd play pom-pom-pullaway (a complex game of tag) or something like that, hide and go seek. And then they had a curfew, so we'd have to be in at eight o'clock or nine o'clock for sure. If you wasn't, the marshall he'd come and he'd see that you got home. But I'd have time for picnics, too. I went on a few picnics. My dad used to take us on a picnic and have a barbecued lamb. We'd go out in the hills, sing a little while, pick some flowers, pick some berries and come home.[6]

Recess at the Old Rock School, 1888

All the old-timers grew up in similar circumstances and remember that there was always something to be done around the house. Some remember more of the difficulties than the pleasures. Josephine Stajduhar, for example, talks about a similarly crowded living space and stresses the hardships of her childhood:

My mother, she only had two bedrooms, for six kids. And then Mom and Dad, they always had a baby sleeping in with them, and then the girls had one room and then my brother had a little bed in the front room. It was hard, kid, but what're you going to do? You didn't enjoy yourself. What little we played, you might as well say we didn't have no time for it. No, we didn't know what good times were. We worked. Like I said, we were oh, about say eight, nine, ten, we were already looking to bring coal and wood home for the winter. We didn't have washing machines. I don't know how old I was, let's see, when Dorothy was born. . . . I had to do her diapers and all her little things, everything on a washboard and everything, before I went to school. We did the dishes, we made our beds, then we did the chores if they wanted us to go here or there to

Joseph H. Block and V. E. Metzler fishing on the Taylor River

do things. There was no pleasure. There was no toys or nothing to play with. We walked, that was on Sundays is all. All week, you was home.[7]

Joe Sedmak agrees that there was little time for relaxation and frivolity: "Them days we didn't have any extra fun." Most of his time was spent doing chores and working: "Hell, we were kids, we went up where the mine was, you'd pick coal in the summer (collecting lumps big enough for use at home that had been discarded with rock from the mine or fallen off coal cars). Of course our parents didn't have any money. I started picking coal when I was about ten years old." Tony Mihelich adds: "We didn't have much recreation. You made your own. It was baseball, mostly, for the boys."[8]

What free time children did have growing up in Crested Butte in the 1910s and 1920s was mostly spent out of doors, hiking and fishing and hunting before the snow came. John Somrak remembers the various activities that the children participated in during the winter:

> Well, I'll tell you, in the wintertime there wasn't much to do, I mean you couldn't do much during the weekdays—school days—then you had chores to do at home, then it was dark. Weekends you had chores to do, then maybe you went sleigh riding or you went skiing. Then in the summertime when school was out, we used to have to haul coal for the coal mines, pick the coal along the railroad track, we'd have to haul all the wood in, saw it, chop it, get it all ready for winter. We used to have to help with the garden . . . take care of the yard, raise rabbits so we'd have something to eat and sell a few and then if you had any other time left over you had to go fishing. . . . We fished just about every other day—the four of us.

Tony says that everybody did a lot of hunting and fishing because "in those days, that's what you survived on."[9]

Lyle McNeill was one of those who was very young when he started work to help support his family. Before he stopped school in the eighth grade when his mother became sick with cancer, he worked in the dairy early in the morning and after classes and peddled milk around town with a team of donkeys. Tony Stefanic also quit school after eighth grade to start delivering for Fisher's Grocery. Fred Yaklich helped his father in the dairy, milking cows and delivering milk, and also sold pastries from the family bakery. Rudy Sedmak worked for a local rancher when he was about twelve, cleaning ditches and fixing fences, and was paid a quart of milk for every day he worked.

The many mine-related deaths introduced children to harsh reality at an early age and greatly added to the hardships of the family. The family was more fortunate if at the time of the father's death there were children old enough to go outside the home for work. When Johnny Krizmanich's father died, for example, his older brothers were fourteen or fifteen, and so were able to help support the family. It was not uncommon for a boy to take on the responsibilities as the head of the household.

Everyone went through periods of individual struggle in Crested Butte. There were also hard times which affected the entire community. The periods of greatest economic difficulty were during long strikes and just following the Great Depression. Johnny Krizmanich says the worst he remembers was when the IWW came to town in 1927. He remembers the strike lasting

Hunting was less a sport than a necessity to provide for the family table.

for about eight months, during which all the families in town were forced to turn to various resources for food: "We'd eat a lot of wild meat, lots of fish, a lot of deer, elk. We ate a lot of sauerkraut, sour turnips. We had credit at the stores."[10]

Crested Butte did not escape the national economic trends. The town began to feel the effects of the Depression around 1931, when the local bank failed. Charles Ross, local business entrepreneur and vice president of the bank, was later found guilty of embezzlement. Everyone in town who had money in the bank lost their savings. Most of the smaller mines, which had already been hurt by national economic trends, closed down as a result of the bank failure;

The Elk Cafe and Bar

even the Big Mine was closed for repairs in 1931 and 1932. Overall, the local economy was made less stable and more dependent upon CF&I.[11]

Fred Yaklich remembers people arriving on the railroad, looking for work: "We had people coming in, they'd ride the railroad cars, do anything just to get a bite to eat. They'd come and ask if you had work. My dad had a bakery then, and they'd come there, chop the wood, carry the coal, anything just for some stale donuts. Just so they had a bite to eat." Despite his own family's hardships, Teeny Tezak remembers mostly the desperate situation of area farmers when 125-pound hogs sold for a dollar:

. . . them poor farmers from around Delta and Olathe . . . they'd be begging them, "Please buy one so I won't have to take it back." And they had them beat up trucks, they didn't have wipers, they didn't have heaters, some of them had windows knocked out and they were driving at night. And they didn't have headlights like they do nowadays. When guys would go pheasant hunting over there, some of them would recognize them and said, "You're from Crested Butte." They'd even go show them where the pheasants were: "If it wouldn't have been for you Crested Butteans, we would've starved to death. You pulled us through and we'll show you where they're at."[12]

In the summer of 1930, Teeny worked for the forest service and was the only member of his family to be employed: "The rates wasn't high, but four dollars a day, that was big money them days. I gave everything to Mama. I'd just sign the check and give it to her. We were paid once a month . . . My stepfather used to cry when I brought that paycheck home, he was so ashamed."[13]

Despite long periods of unemployment, however, it seems that no one went hungry. All the families knew how to get by on very little. Betty Spehar describes: "As I said, nobody starved. And the housewife, even if she cooked very inexpensive meals, she would cook them well. Corn meal mush with good dressing or good gravy, or pastas, risottos, dumplings."[14] Josephine Stajduhar says that during the summertime, "That's all we had. Potatoes, lettuce and fish. And they went hunting illegally, to get the game. There was no money for licenses." They tired of the same food, as Josephine shows in joking

Communion class, 1907

The Shuster Band. Music was one of the most important elements of the Old Country heritage and was important in day-to-day life as well as holidays and celebrations.

with her sister Helen: "You told Mama—maybe you don't remember, but you said to her, 'Mama — fish every meal, pretty soon I'm going to look like a damn fish, but I can't swim!'"[15]

Essential to everyone's well-being during those times was the system of credit in the stores, usually interest-free. Tony Mihelich remembers how important this credit was during the major coal strikes: "There wasn't no income of any kind at the time, just some tough times to get through. And of course they didn't have welfare at the time. Credit is what let the people exist. That was the only way they could exist from week to week."[16]

Only in such a small community where everyone knew each other and relied upon the support of one another could this system of credit have worked. It could be risky for the store owners because they were never sure when or if they would be paid back. June Krizmanich worked for Tony Stefanic for seventeen years, however, and says he always found people trustworthy:

Mr. & Mrs. V. E. Metzler prepare to go skiing

"He always said that people were really honest, you know . . . not like now . . . back further, he said if people owed him a bill and they even left town, he said usually they'd send him the money. . . ."[17]

Betty Spehar remembers people coming to her after her father had died to say that he had saved their lives by allowing them so much credit at his store. There was an interdependency in the community that ensured people would never go hungry and guaranteed them help in times of suffering, as Betty describes:

> There may have been a few people that wouldn't know how to manage, but neighbors chipped in. And if anyone was ill, they would always be helped. And the lodges, of course, did that, too . . . you know, someone would say, "Well I'm taking the wash this week" or, "I'll take it today." And they would informally organize a support group to take care of people in trouble. And the lodges set up a system for sitting with people who were ill. Someone was there through the night if the person was in danger of death or something. They went and took hours, say, one hour at a time, got up in the middle of the night and went to be there with the sick person.[18]

Despite the support provided for people by the community, some old-timers remember the bitter personal struggle more than anything else and

Funeral procession with fraternal lodge members, early 1920s

speak of the past in terms of their own successes and self-improvement. John Somrak, for example, describes his years in the mines in terms of having to "buck the system" and work his way up from the bottom. He says what gave him "the most satisfaction" was taking on the responsibility of raising his two younger half brothers after his stepfather died. John describes with pride how, at the age of eleven, he declared he would take care of them: "I said, 'I'll tell you one thing, I'm going to raise Josie and Frankie. I have a piece of bread and I'm going to break it three ways. Josie gets one, Frankie gets one, I get one.'" John mostly sees his life as one man's efforts to get by in the face of a series of hardships, and he disputes the notion that it was a warm and supportive community:

Funeral procession with fraternal lodge flags encased in black

There were good and bad. You know, Crested Butte wasn't like you heard that old story and still hear it—"one big family." Like hell! It was dog-eat-dog. "One big family?" I know I went through that. I went through the Depression and I went through the whole damn works. I know exactly what Crested Butte was, what the people were like up there and their religions and the Ku Klux Klans and the Protestants and the whole smear—the scabs in the coal mine and the company thugs that come in there and shoot people that was on strike and all that stuff. I know all that, so they ain't telling me what the hell Crested Butte was.[19]

For most, though, Crested Butte was special because it was home. The Krizmaniches speak of the comforting simplicity of life in a small town where people were dedicated to their families and to their community. When asked if Crested Butte differed from anywhere else, Johnny said: "Special, sure. It's home, you know. Home's always special. A lot of them people that left there and moved to different places, they still call Crested Butte home." June adds: "There's deep ties there. I don't know why."[20]

Laundry was usually done on Monday and hung on lines strung through pulleys on high poles to avoid winter snow deposits. The coke ovens, which produced dirty smoke, were often shut down that day to ensure clean clothes.

It seems that there was something special about the people that lived in Crested Butte: "Nice people's all I can say," says Johnny. "If you was a good-time Charlie they were your friends, and if you was down in the—lowest person in the world, they were still your friends."[21]

The consensus is that it was an unusual community because everyone experienced similar hardships—whether it was family tragedy or economic strain—and because people supported each other through difficult times. Everyone knew everyone, families stayed together and people helped each other if they could. Teeny Tezak says what he appreciated was "just the way people lived. It was more like one family. In hard times, one'd help the other out." Margaret Malensek remembers how everyone got along: "We was like one big great family, the whole bunch of us. If anything happened to anybody, it happened to everybody. If they had sorrows, it was everybody's sorrows; if it was a joy, it was everybody's joy. It was just all flung together."[22]

The fact that nearly everyone in Crested Butte was of the same economic standing contributed to the overall sense of camaraderie. As Betty Spehar says, "There was no real wealth, so nobody was economically class conscious, no. As long as people kept their heads above water and paid their bills, and kept their homes and their families together, everybody was on top." People's shared experience and community closeness transcended all ethnic boundaries as well. Josephine says:

> We all stuck together. It didn't matter what you were. They all talked to you, respected you, were nice and all. They were all treated the same. 'Cause they were all hard-working people, and no one was better than the other. No one had any more than you did. It was really nice.[23]

"Colorado—a snow-slide on Crested Butte, of the Elk Mountain Range, 1884"

The one thing the mining town of the past and the ski town of the present have in common is the snow . . .

The old-timers say that winters today are nothing like they used to be. Beginning in September and ending in May, winter in Crested Butte always seemed to last forever, bringing severe snow storms and consistently below-zero temperatures. The first snowfall usually came around Labor Day and by Christmas there was a solid base of at least two to three feet. From the beginning of December through the month of January, the temperatures in town dropped every night to $-10°$ to $-40°$ Fahrenheit. February brought warmer temperatures and heavier snowfall; in March the snowmelt began and was interrupted by an occasional blizzard. The snow around town was not completely gone until May.

During these long winter months, the stoves in every little house were kept going twenty four hours a day, and clouds of black smoke hovered over the town, filling the thin mountain air with the sickly sweet odor of burning coal. Houses were literally buried by snow, as storms came over the mountains or up the valley and descended upon the small town and its expectant inhabitants. Sometimes blizzards lasted for days at a time.

The task of shovelling was never finished. People had to be constantly clearing a path from their doorways to the streets if they wanted to leave their

Train with a rotary snowplow. This plow, invented in 1883, was powerful, but snow was frequently so deep that only shovelling by the crew could clear the track. Passengers, tired of waiting, often helped.

houses. And there was always the danger of roofs and windows caving in under the immense weight of the snow unless they were shovelled on a regular basis. Sometimes people would have to get up in the middle of the night just to shovel off their roofs. Neglect of this duty could have disastrous consequences. Joe Sedmak recalls that seven buildings collapsed in the winter of 1951–1952. Joe Saya remembers shovelling more snow that winter than ever before:

> We had seventy two inches of snow fall in twenty four hours . . . it was nine feet deep on the level . . . that's the most amount of snow I remember up there in Crested Butte. I think that's the most any of them remember. . . . I had to shovel my way out to the street and leave my shovel out there . . . so when I come home from work I could shovel my way into the house. If you didn't keep your house shovelled, your house might cave in . . . You had to be on your house in that winter just about every day, just to keep shovelling. I've got a picture in front of my house, the snow's so deep it covered the arch right at my gate where you go through. That's how deep the snow was. Like I say, it was nine feet deep.[1]

The clearing of the snow was done either by hand or with the help of horses that were used to drag old rails through the streets, pushing the snow to one side. Travel in the wintertime was very slow, if not impossible. As Joe Sedmak says, ". . . they didn't plow the streets or nothing. If you had a car, about the first of October you put it in the garage, jacked it up, took off the tires . . . in May you put them back on and drove the car again." Leola tells of her hus-

"Snowshoers" at Irwin, March 1883. Early skis were 9 to 14 feet long, held on by leather straps and used for transportation. Single "guide poles" were used to steady or steer.

band's trials delivering milk from his dairy in the snow: "In the winter, he'd take a horse with a little sled with his milk cans to go up that hill. And if the horse got off the trail, he had to shovel the horse out!"[2]

Crested Butte was always isolated—and still is—because of its distance from other towns and its location at the end of a valley, surrounded on three sides by mountains. Before the days of mechanized snow removal, it was not uncommon for Crested Butte to lose contact completely with the outside world, especially when trains were prevented from coming to town. Sometimes the tracks were blocked for weeks at a time, as Joe Sedmak remembers:

"Hell, they said that a couple times the train couldn't even come for twenty days or so." And if the trains did not make it up the valley, the mines could not operate: ". . . we'd go to work in the mornings when it snowed two or three feet, get in the mine, and they'd tell us that we couldn't work that day 'cause the train can't get in to bring the railroad cars. So we'd have to go home again to wait for them to plow the track."[3]

Sleigh riding, snowshoeing, and skiing were all popular wintertime activities, especially among children. Lyle McNeill remembers the fun he had as a child riding around on the hardened top layer of snow: ". . . when the snow was crust, there'd be forty five or fifty of us and we'd go over to Crested Butte

Mountain and sleigh ride. You could look out there at night and you could see three, four, five big bonfires going. And that was nothing but children up there sleigh riding. They had a wonderful time."4

Skiing was also popular, but with none of the conveniences that today's skiers enjoy. Joe Saya describes skiing when he was a boy as an ordeal:

> In them days, the skis were just old boards or something, or we'd call them barrel staves. If you found some leather strap or something to nail to them, that's what you called your skis. . . . There was some fellow up there used to make skis, a dollar and a half was a good pair of skis, made out of pine . . . and if you'd go over a hump, your skis'd break.5

Even if the skier made it down the slope without breaking or losing a ski, there was no lift to bring him back up to the top: "When you wanted to ski, you'd have to buck snow up the hill, and it wasn't a very big hill either. And you'd ski down there, and when you'd climbed once or twice up that hill, you didn't ski very much." Tony Mihelich also recollects the difficulties of skiing: "We *walked* up the hill. We had big long skis in them days, not these fancy ones they got nowadays. We didn't have any boots, just some hold straps. And we went straight down the hill, no

John Somrak shovelling his walk

turns or anything. If you got two, three runs, we used to call it a day." The lack of comfortable equipment and the absence of any means of getting to the top of the slope other than one's own two feet dissuaded the most avid of skiers from taking more than a few runs at a time.[6]

The younger people who live in Crested Butte today also say that the winters can be very harsh and long. The town can still be shut down by heavy snowfall and extreme temperatures. Pipes freeze, telephone lines go down, and streets go temporarily unplowed. Constant shovelling is still required, since pathways are needed and roofs continue to be vulnerable to collapse. By the time April arrives, people are longing for spring.

Despite the complaints toward the end of a long winter, however, there is no doubt that snow is the most valuable resource in today's Crested Butte. It brings the skiers and their support to the local economy. The amount of snow and when it falls largely determines whether the season will be a good one. Colorado daily newspapers print the inches of snowfall in every ski area, and these reports are consulted by skiers before they choose where they will spend their vacations. A season with too little snow can be disastrous, forcing small businesses to close and depressing the entire town's economy.

The skiers also rely on the quality of deep powder, for which Colorado ski areas are justly famous. Dedicated enthusiasts of the sport respond joyously when the forecast is for snow. Rising early so that they can be the first on the lifts, they fit as many trips down the mountain into the day as they can, echoing the popular refrain, "just one more run," until the lifts close in the late afternoon. Avid skiers think nothing of riding up the Paradise lift in

January with a wind-chill factor of −80° Fahrenheit in order to slalom across wide open bowls through soft, plush powder. At the end of the kind of day that the Rockies are known for, with freshly fallen snow, blue skies, and bright sunshine, the most commonly heard description of the day's skiing is, simply,

Early snow-making machine, 1970s

"awesome." Whereas before locals worried that there would be too much snow, the constant fear today is that there will not be enough. Rather than dissuading people from settling in Crested Butte, the snow is now the reason why so many of them come.

IV

SKI TOWN

TRANSFORMATION

In August of 1952, the CF&I Big Mine, which had provided fairly steady employment and pay to Crested Butte for nearly sixty years, permanently shut down. All of its miners were unemployed overnight; the community splintered. Any hope of the mine reopening disappeared when the D&RG railroad pulled its narrow gauge tracks in 1954.

In some ways, the closing of the mine should not have come as a surprise. Coal production in Colorado had been gradually diminishing since its record boom during the Second World War. After the War, the output of the Big Mine steadily declined, as did Crested Butte's population; the single miners, who were generally the most transient segment of the population, were the first to leave.[1]

According to the U.S. Census, the population dropped from 1,213 in 1920 to 730 in 1950, a loss of forty percent of its residents. When the Big Mine closed, the population dropped an additional sixty percent, dwindling to only 289 in 1960. The best and largest deposits of coal around Crested Butte had been exhausted, and the high cost of transporting it to market discouraged further production as people looked for cheaper fuel closer to home. Moreover, natural gas, electricity, and oil were replacing coal as major energy sources.[2]

Elk Avenue in the 1950s

There had always been rumors that the Big Mine would close; as Eleanor Stefanic says, "They were closing that mine from the day I came here. The rumor was going around, 'The mine's going to close, the mine's going to close.' And then finally it happened." Tony adds: "They were operating that way for sixty eight years. So it was quite a shock to the town." The end came as a bewildering blow to the miners and their families. As Lyle McNeill says, "That was a very, very depressing day. Because none of us really knew what it was all about. We really didn't know what the future was for Crested Butte." Margaret Malensek felt the same way: "It was a sad day. We knew it was going to be like a ghost town. Everybody sold, some went to Denver, some went to Pueblo, some moved to Gunnison, so we all scattered."[3]

The Slogar Bar, 1971

To Josephine Stajduhar, the saddest part was seeing all of her friends leave:

> They're all gone. They all moved all over. Most of them went to Denver, Pueblo, Trinidad, Paonia, Somerset, all where the coal mines were. That's all the work they knew, see? It was really sad, sad to see them leave. Nobody even told you they were leaving, they just picked up and left. And now when they come visit you for a day or two, my god, you're in seventh heaven.

Most of the families moved down to Pueblo to work in the CF&I steel mills where the miners had been offered jobs by the company.[4]

To those few who decided they would remain in Crested Butte, the years that followed the closing of the Big Mine brought uncertainty and instability.

No one knew what was going to happen to the town. Teeny Tezak "just thought it was finished," and Eleanor Stefanic supposed it would be "more or less of a ghost town because there were no tourists then."⁵

The closing affected people in different ways, depending on where they were working at the time. The miners, of course, were hardest hit, since the only job most of them ever knew was no longer available. The Stefanics say they had too much tied up in the store to be able to afford to just get up and leave. And Tony Mihelich stayed even though the future of his business was uncertain: "I didn't have no incentive to stay. I just hoped that by staying, eventually with more tourists coming in, I would be able to make a living."⁶

John's Store, 1960s

Some of the miners who decided they would stay in Crested Butte were fortunate to already have other jobs and so did not have to move away. Teeny Tezak, for example, was working on the railroad: "Everybody had to decide what they were going to do. It didn't bother me because I already had a job. You see, I quit the mines before they closed." Teeny also did not have a family of his own to worry about. Lyle McNeill was fortunate to be working for the county in the highway department. And Fred Yaklich was running the local dairy, which he managed to keep going until 1960.⁷

Of the miners who suddenly found themselves without jobs, some decided they had enough of mining and looked for other work. Joe Saya was determined not to go back to the mines; in his words, "I was through with

mining." He spent several winters in other states to find work, traveling to Oklahoma City and various places in California. Despite his travels, in the end he always returned: "I always came back home . . . good old Crested Butte."

John Somrak was also determined to get out of mining: "I was still in the mines and I realized my Dad got killed in there, a lot of other people got killed in there, a lot of my friends got injured and I says, 'hard work—if I ever get out of there, I'm going to find myself something different.'" He went on to take several different jobs in Gunnison and eventually went to work for the U.S. Forest Service.[8]

Other miners, like Johnny Krizmanich, decided they would continue to mine wherever they could find work, even though their families would remain in Crested Butte. Johnny was separated from his family and home for long periods of time and spent the rest of his working life moving from job to job. For a while, he worked in the Keystone Mine and Mill, on the side of Mt.

Emmons three miles west of Crested Butte, but most of the time he was forced to leave Crested Butte to find employment. He went to work in Pueblo, where CF&I had other coal mines and steel mills, and in Carbondale.

Many people from Crested Butte were in Pueblo and a few, including one of Johnny's older brothers, were in Carbondale. None of the work he found was very dependable, and he was often forced to take jobs he did not like. He even spent some time working for the Coors brewery in Golden, which is five hours away by car. About working in the brewery, he said: "I didn't care too much for it. I got laid off twice. People that were the last hired were the ones that got laid off. And then Golden wasn't a very friendly town. In Crested Butte everybody knew everybody, you know. And the work wasn't near as hard work as mining." Johnny's strong ties to Crested Butte prevented him from moving away permanently as others did; instead, June stayed here with their son John and he commuted home on the weekends.⁹

Right after the mine shut down, Rudy Sedmak did various jobs

Tony Stefanic in front of his store, 1975

Kochevar houses, 1971

around town, including carpentry and construction, but did not like the inconsistency of the work. He moved around for several years, doing construction on Indian reservations in New Mexico and Arizona, working for the Thompson Mine in Carbondale and living in Glenwood Springs, where he and his wife also ran the food counter at Brian's Drug Store, and working as the caretaker of an estate in Aspen. Rudy considered Crested Butte home during those years and came back to live as soon as he could. Why did he not move away permanently? "I just didn't want to leave. I was going to be Judd—the last man to leave Crested Butte."[10] Judd was the last miner to live in the town of Gothic years after everyone else had left. Judd Falls was named for him.

Many women and children stayed in Crested Butte, while the men went away to find work. The population dwindled considerably in size, to no more than two hundred people; as Leola Yaklich recalls, "It was like a graveyard, really, at night." Despite the lack of employment or any dependable future, however, many remember the small community as being more supportive

during those years than ever before. After having been away at school, Betty Spehar returned to Crested Butte just before the mine closed. In her words, "My philosophy was, if the town's going to die, I'm going to be there, holding its hand." She taught English at the high school and junior high school for five years and describes that time as being a very special period in the town's life: "Those were very beautiful years, those five years. Because, again, still, enough people were beautifully loving; and, though we were isolated, we had a grand time."[11]

Crested Butte did not die. Many houses were left empty, and at night there were few lights to be seen in the dark streets of the town, but enough families remained to keep the school in operation and a few businesses

New ski area 1963–1964 with Malensek Ranch buildings on the right

stayed, including Stefanic's and Tony's Crested Butte Hardware and Auto Supply. It soon became clear, however, that the closing of the Big Mine and the events that immediately followed were just the first in a series of major changes to which Crested Butte natives would have to adjust. With its location at the end of one of the most beautiful valleys in Colorado, surrounded on three sides by open mountain country, it slowly became apparent that Crested Butte's destiny was to become a prime tourist and recreation area.

The first outsiders to come into town, aside from the small number of seasonal tourists who came primarily to fish, were employed by the American Smelting and Refining Company in the Keystone Mine and Mill. The mine produced lead, zinc, copper, and silver from 1952 until it closed in 1969. The Keystone hired some coal miners, like Johnny Krizmanich, but most of its

Father McKenna blessing the first gondola in 1961

employees came from elsewhere and were different from the miners of Crested Butte: "There's a lot of difference between hard-rock mining and coal mining." Tony Mihelich remembers different work and different people. "They were always looking for a mine that was better or had better conditions." Leola Yaklich also remembers the hard-rock miners as restless people who did not want to settle down: "A lot of them came and they had to go again. They lived much more for today. They had a saying, they themselves, 'Chicken today, feathers tomorrow.'" Fred adds:

The hard-rockers, they made pretty good money and if they made good money they'd stay, but if they weren't making it, they'd head for another place where they heard, you know, they're making big money in Utah or Montana. They'd pick up and go. Yeah, they were different. Like I say, "Chicken today, feathers tomorrow" and "the only good mine is the one you left."[12]

The first new business endeavor in town outside of mining was the Law-Science Academy started in the 1950s by Dr. Hubert Winston Smith, a lawyer and doctor from Oklahoma City. Smith bought several old buildings in town for very little money and based the summertime academy in the old Croatian Hall. The academy drew a small, varied group of participants to town for one month out of the summer and held sessions that were open to the public. The fifty to sixty attendees with their families had a positive if limited impact on the local economy.

Rudy Sedmak worked for Dr. Smith for twelve years, collecting rent on Smith's thirty eight properties. He describes Smith as "a very brilliant man, but when it come to knowing the simple things in life, he wasn't there."[13]

According to George Sibley, who was editor of the town newspaper at the time, Smith had a "high culture" vision for Crested Butte, similar to that of the Aspen Institute. It was, however, says Sibley, a vision to be fulfilled according to Smith's own rules and had nothing to do with other newcomers or the old-timers. The academy folded in 1971. Most of the old-timers had little contact with Smith; only a few attended any of the sessions.[14]

The 1960s were the transitional years for the town of Crested Butte. The important business venture was the opening of the ski area. It was a development that would set off a pattern of continual change, permanently altering the landscape of the town and the kind of people who wanted to live there.

In 1960 two Kansans, Dick Eflin and Fred Rice, bought the old Malensek Ranch located three miles north of town. Construction started a year later, and by the winter of 1961–1962, the ski area was in operation with a T-bar and rope tow borrowed from Western State College. Coincidentally, the ski area of Vail opened with much fanfare the same season, so Crested Butte did not receive the attention it might have. In 1966, Eflin sold his interests to his partner who had investments in several other projects at that time. When one of Rice's investments ceased to provide him with income, in Eflin's words, "the castle started to crumble." The ski area was forced into bankruptcy and operated under receivership for the next few years.[15]

In 1970, the ski development was sold to the Crested Butte Development Corporation formed by Howard "Bo" Callaway from Georgia and his brother-in-law Ralph Walton. Callaway had the capital necessary to carry the ski area through downturns in the economy and slow seasons. A separate town of Mt. Crested Butte was incorporated in November 1973 because the issues the ski area was facing were seen to be different from those of the county, and the developers did not want to be restrained by county regulations.

Today Crested Butte is a transformed town. Physically, it is expanding outward across the valley floor and up the sides of the surrounding slopes. Thirty-foot-high buildings dominate streets where once there were only single-story miners' houses, and most of the houses that remained have been renovated into cute, colorful, picture-perfect homes. There are sidewalks on Elk Avenue, and the streets in town are paved and plowed throughout the winter. The town supports at least twenty restaurants, several of which serve expensive, gourmet food. Almost all major buildings have been renovated, and some of the most frequented stores in town are tee-shirt and souvenir shops that cater to visitors.

Crested Butte experiences the population fluctuations typical of a tourist town. The year-round population in 1994 was estimated by the Chamber of Commerce to have been 1,456, only recently surpassing its 1920 peak of 1,213. Mt. Crested Butte, located three miles up the road at the base of the Crested Butte Mountain, experiences significantly more seasonal fluctuation. According to the 1990 census, Mt. Crested Butte's population was 336. Its capacity,

however, is much greater than its population indicates; in 1993, it had 1,664 housing units, which include hotel rooms, condominiums, and houses.[16]

Those skiers that stay up on the mountain are brought into the town of Crested Butte by a bus shuttle that runs back and forth regularly. The two towns, so close to one another and both dependent upon tourism in the ski season, have little else in common. There is a small and growing community in Mt. Crested Butte, but aside from the few conventions that are held there in the summertime, it exists primarily for the skiers. Its population is comprised mostly of people who own second homes and of "ski bums" who come to the area for only a season or two, with the intention of working just enough so that they can ski as much as possible. The town of Crested Butte provides the community center for the entire area. Those who live there tend to distinguish themselves from the tourists and the ski area residents and consider Crested Butte to be the focal point of the valley.

The immediate benefit of the ski area was that it provided employment for many of the old-timers. Rudy Sedmak was the first operator of the T-Bar, which he ran for fifteen years. He later moved over to the Keystone chair, which was also called "Rudy's Lift."[17]

Reny Stajduhar and Johnny Krizmanich did construction work and ran tows, and Lyle McNeill's heavy equipment business helped to put in some of the first lifts. Fred Yaklich and Willard Ruggera went into business and did construction work together and then went into plumbing; for several years they were the only plumbers in town and did all of the early work up at the ski area. Josephine Stajduhar and other women cleaned rooms in the first lodge up on the mountain.

Because it gave them jobs, the old-timers first regarded the ski area in practical terms. As Betty Spehar says, "When the first ski promoters came in, they were welcomed because we needed to have something." Josephine appreciated the fact that she and her husband were again able to make a living in Crested Butte: "Well, I liked it, because he was getting his bread and butter up there. So I had to like it." And even though he did not like the work because it was so different from what he was used to, Johnny Krizmanich also recognizes that it provided him with an income.[18]

Tony Mihelich states simply: "It was good for business." John Somrak says it was "the best damn thing that ever happened to Crested Butte." And Lyle McNeill, who enjoyed the work he did up there, says it was "a great thing." He saw that the ski area development would revive the local economy and provide people with a means of making a living. Because of it, he feels the town survived: "Any change that you can make that's going to help the people as a whole—families, and stuff like that—this is what they need. And a place that doesn't have change and progress, it becomes dormant."[19]

THE NEW PEOPLE

Old-timers agree that the ski area saved Crested Butte from becoming a ghost town, but the development on the mountain soon brought changes that were unfamiliar and troublesome. The most significant one proved to be not the ski area itself, or the scarring of Crested Butte Mountain; rather, it was the new people who came into this small community with little or no understanding of those who lived there and had made Crested Butte what it was.

Johnny Krizmanich says simply that the newcomers were "a different kind of people." He believes a lot of them felt they were superior to the natives: "It seemed like at that period of time we were getting a lot of these very highly educated people who thought they were much better than the coal miners. And then we had the hippie element."

Although some of the old-timers welcomed strangers and others did not, all agree that the "hippie element," which started to arrive in the late 1960s and remained a strong presence through the mid-1970s, was the most difficult to accept. Their way of life, as Josephine Stajduhar describes it, was very foreign to the old-timers:

> The only thing that was really bad was when all the filthy, you know, hippies came in. Oh, kid, it was terrible. They were so dirty. Ooooh,

they're human, yes but, kid, they were so filthy dirty, their hair was long and matted, and . . . ohhh, it just turned my stomach. Because we were used to being clean, everything nice, you know, and when you seen them, *awww*. And all their dogs they brought in? Uh uh![1]

According to many of the old-timers, the hippies had little or no respect for private property. They lived off Social Security checks and food stamps, and they stayed almost anywhere they could find a place to lie down. June Krizmanich agrees that the hippies were hard to deal with: "They were really bad, the first bunch." June regularly came into contact with everyone in town through her job at Stefanic's and remembers her first encounters with the new people. They were different from the customers she was used to: "Some of them were really obnoxious, and cussing and everything. Some of them kids that had started at the ski area, they just didn't care, you know, what they said in front of you or anything — where an old-timer would never do that." June also had to endure her new neighbors by herself while her husband Johnny was away working in Paonia:

Pitching horseshoes in the Grubstake Beer Garden, 1970s

One night young John and I were home by ourselves and about one o'clock in the morning we heard noise like somebody pounding. We went outside and could see into the house next door. The kids were on dope and they were hitting the fridge with a hammer and breaking the windows and everything. We got scared so we called the cops and they came over and stopped them. They were a rough, rough bunch.[2]

Josephine Stajduhar had similar experiences:

I remember you'd go up to the post office or to the store, and people, they thought they *owned* the sidewalks and the streets. You had to move for them. They wouldn't move for you. It was awful. I don't know if they think it's like the city, because they say in the city people bump into each other, they don't talk to anybody else. So if they think this is a great big city, well I don't look at it that way. They're in the wrong place. And you go any place, and if you try to go in, you have to hold the door for the men. He won't hold it for you. You gotta let him in first. But if a man comes, if I go to the bank, I'll hold the door for him. I'll show him that I'm a lady. They're not going to take what was taught to me, take that away from me.[3]

Hippies on the Company Store bench, 1970s

Other old-timers remember those who behaved in this extreme fashion as being only a small portion of the newcomers. Tony Mihelich recalls that "Some of them were quite a nuisance in the town," but that "a lot of people here didn't like them; even the tourists noticed them." Leola Yaklich says that for the most part the new young people were very pleasant, even if they did lead an unusual kind of life:

> Now my reaction to the hippies was entirely different. There were a few that were strange. But you can't generalize something, you know. So many of them were so nice to the older people. They were so accommodating . . . and would do anything they could for them. To me, they just weren't that bad. I don't quite understand some people's reactions. Maybe it was just because it was something different. They didn't want the change. And of course they weren't used to that type of young person. They just weren't. The hippies were different, admittedly. They didn't keep their houses as clean as the ladies here were used to.[4]

Gwen Danni describes what separated the new people and the old: "Different ideas, I think. Your old are a lunch bucket group of people. They lived off the land . . . and the new generation, they just make their living completely different, so things don't mean the same to them. And with the old-timers, that's where your friction is."

Johnny Krizmanich's feelings exemplify how perplexing the attitudes of the new people were, saying about his own life: "We were just poor people. You know, all the people who worked in mines like that were poor people. June's people weren't any better off than mine. We were poor people and we stayed poor." And he described working in the mines as "a good hard honest living." The values of those who did not have to work, or did not want to, who were in town only to play, were incomprehensible.[5]

Many of the new arrivals had no interest in a traditional way of life—settling down, getting a job, and raising a family. One reason is that the tourist industry in Crested Butte, especially in its early years, could not support steady jobs, but few had any intention of staying in Crested Butte anyway; the majority were merely passing through. As Matt Malensek points out, this transiency, which continues to be an aspect of the community, was very dissimilar from the way the old-timers lived:

> The old-timers, they had to stay put. The newcomers, some of them bring a dollar or two, and they'd start a business. When the dollars are gone, the man is gone with them. There was many a place started up there, but there ain't too many of them stayed. They had to go.[6]

Many of the old-timers still believe that the greatest distinction between themselves and the new people is their work ethic. Some do not have steady jobs. And the jobs they do have, from waiting tables to white-collar jobs, differ radically from the physical labor of mining. Matt Malensek describes the newcomers as unwilling to work hard for their money: "Everybody's looking for something for nothing, see if you can get a job that you don't have to work . . . that's the attitude they got nowadays. There ain't nobody thinking about how much am I going to do. It's how little can I get by with."[7]

Josephine Stajduhar expresses dissatisfaction with those who came and took over her town and criticizes their unwillingness to settle down: "For me, now, I don't want to have nothing to do with these people—strangers. They just come and go." She feels alienated from the younger people, "because their life is different than ours." And they have none of the values with which she was raised: ". . . they don't believe in sitting home and trying to save and do what's right. They just want to go for good times. It's just all good times. That's why they named it a fun town. A bunch of them went by and they said 'Boy, they never seen such a place; it sure is a fun town.'"[8]

Fred Yaklich comments on what he perceives to be the major difference between his generation and later generations: "The difference in those days, you know, it was work and no play. Now it's play and no work." Leola Yaklich agrees that many of the younger people in town seem to live only for the purpose of recreation:

Music stage at the Arts Fair, 1970s

"Before, we had to work for whatever we could get. Now kids come in and are ski bums and live any way they can. It seems to be their whole life."[9]

Josephine says that because of the comfort and ease young people enjoy today, they would never survive the life that she led: "Like I said, if somebody . . . some of these other boys and girls, if they had to go through what we did, they wouldn't make it. They wouldn't make it."[10] Tony Stefanic agrees:

Hot dogger, 1970s

Everybody wants to go to college today. All right, if everybody wants to go to college, who's going to work?. . . And the ones who've been to college are all running around trying to see if they can make a fast buck. That's about all I can see out of it. They say, "Oh we're going to be here for a year, two, six years," first thing you hear so-and-so moved. The older people my age, when we got married we raised our family, we run our business. . . . These days I see kids twenty, twenty five years old, been around the world. "Good god," I says, "I never even dreamt at that age of going around the world. I don't know what the hell you do." We know two or three of them done that. What it looks to me like, these kids have been brought up and they're plain spoiled. . . . You want to know the truth? I don't think they know how to cut it. I really don't think they know how to cut it. They're just brought up in a different way. They don't believe in a lot of work, they're out more for good times and you don't find people who are going to do much good. You gotta find people who want to work. . . . They just don't have any intention of working.[11]

Earliest days of the mountain bike era—
jumping contest on Elk Avenue in the 1970s

In an effort to explain the sometimes puzzling freedom that the new people enjoy, many of the old-timers attribute it to money. Rudy Malensek says:

There's more money floating around than there was in them days. There wasn't no money. If somebody gave you a nickel, you thought you had something. They'd throw it at you, if you offered a kid a nickel now."[12]

His wife, Margaret, agrees that money causes the younger people to develop questionable values:

It's a different generation altogether. The people all think differently. We were people that was brought up to save. People nowadays, they got credit cards, they don't care if they save or just live from today to tomorrow, and they don't care what the next day brings. We always looked ahead. People don't look ahead now, like I said.[13]

With credit cards, Margaret and Eleanor point out, people can spend what they do not have, and therefore do not feel the same pressure to have steady incomes. Or, Teeny Tezak says, they are just accustomed to the way the government helps people with unemployment benefits, a form of assistance that did not exist when he was younger:

In olden times, you didn't have that. Your work was all, otherwise you didn't have no income. See, if that Social Security was run like I was brought up, that was for the elderly and disabled only. If you was safe to go to work, you couldn't get relief.[14]

Joe Sedmak adds that many of the skiers do not need to work because they have outside sources of income: "I say that most of the kids in this town, they're mostly 'trust fund babies.' You see lots of them go to the post office and say, 'Oh, my mom sent me a hundred dollars.' Or two hundred. They're getting a check and they never work." Teeny concludes Crested Butte as a tourist area draws a very different kind of people: "Mostly what they call ski bums. They travel and stay for a while at one ski area and then travel to another ski area . . . Like I say, more modern times of living."[15]

THE POWER SHIFT

Some of the newcomers that arrived in the 1970s came to stay. Many of those were college-educated easterners several generations younger than the old-timers. Largely in reaction to the political upheaval that surrounded the Vietnam war, they sought refuge from what they perceived to be societal ill, and escape from the aggravations and restrictions of urban life. They found in Crested Butte an idyllic haven, the perfect place to create a new existence for themselves.

As different from the developers on the mountain as they were from the residents of the town, the new people were liberal and antigrowth. They soon realized it was in their interest to address the challenge of promoting a healthy tourist economy without sacrificing the qualities of the community that they had learned to cherish. Soon a transfer of power and governance began.

Lyle McNeill had been mayor for most of twenty six years before he was beaten by newcomer Bill Crank in 1972. Lyle had seen the need for change to get the economy moving in Crested Butte; he opened a town meeting in 1968, by saying: "We have called this meeting to give the people of this town a chance to say whether they want the town to get up and go or just sit still." But it was not until the new government came in that the agenda shifted entirely to concerns related to tourism.[1]

Joe Sedmak explains the major differences between the new government and the old: "There's Lyle McNeill, he ruled the town for about twenty five years. Nobody cared to run against him. The town, if they spent a thousand dollars a year they was lucky. After the new people came in, the town started doing more. When the ski area came in, there was more people and money coming in."

The other difference was the generational one. In a 1973 report, the average age of those who participated in local government was twenty to thirty years. At that point, the old-timers were in their fifties and sixties.²

The Town Council hired a planning firm, BKR Associates, in January 1973. Made up of Bruce Baumgartner, Jim Kuziak, and Myles Rademan, the firm's mission was "to study the town's growth problems and make a planning report which is instrumental in the obtainment of federal funds for town projects." Rademan made many official declarations of the government's vision of Crested Butte's future; he summed it up as "a green vision, focusing on sustainability, historic preservation, protection of lands, an economy based on recreation, keeping growth in check, anti-real estate and

Hands-on Mayor Lyle McNeill putting up new street signs, 1969

anti-development." It was a vision, finally, of a town "based on a community and the uniqueness of an area, with a past leading gently into the future."[3]

Rademan, along with Bill Crank and others, was one of what are sometimes referred to as the "fathers" of modern-day Crested Butte. He described the transfer of power which occurred in 1972 and the

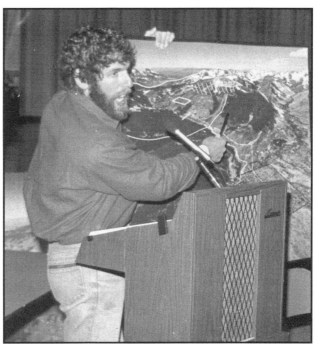

Town planner Myles Rademan

Bruce Baumgartner of
BKR Associates, 1975

general relationship between the old-timers and newcomers like himself as "an entire cultural clash" with a "clear delineation—ethnically, culturally, every which way." Before the change in government, says Rademan, Crested Butte was in no way prepared for the challenges of development and growth; with a population of 300 in 1972, "Crested Butte was an anachronism, something that America had passed by."[4]

Some old-timers, like Joe Saya, also recognize that the government had never had many responsibilities because life was so much simpler when the mines were operating: "There's a different town government now than in mining days. In mining days, the government didn't have nothing much to do. Nothing but talk a lot. Now they got different things they're building, and they're doing different stuff than they used to before."[5]

In order to accomplish what they desired in a short period of time, the government adopted Home Rule in 1975. Whereas before the town could exercise only those powers explicitly granted by the state, now it could do anything set forth in the home rule charter as long as there were no conflicts with state law. This change meant that the government had more flexibility to structure itself, greater authority in zoning and land use, and broader powers of taxation.[6]

Home Rule was passed by the people of Crested Butte but opposed by most of the old-timers. As John Somrak says, "They just didn't want outsiders coming in and taking the town over. But what are they going to do? The old-timers didn't do anything because they didn't have any money to do it with and they didn't know how the hell to get it. And they didn't want to raise taxes, so what?"

Some feel, as Josephine Stajduhar does, that "Home Rule wrecked Crested Butte."[7] Many of the old-timers saw Home Rule as another selfish move by the new people to get what they wanted. Fred Yaklich believes the town manager has too much power, and adds: "There's a lot of things they do that the county wouldn't allow them to do, or wouldn't go for. It was your mill levy and all that was set by the county. Now it's set by Home Rule."

Jim Kuziak of BKR Associates, 1979

The government proceeded to make changes that were thought suitable to a ski town and tourist area, including a new sewer system, better roads, and a general face-lift of the town. To pay for the changes, taxes were raised and the cost of living went up very quickly. Old-timers suddenly had to pay more to the town government for developments they had always lived without quite contentedly.[8]

Many, like Fred Yaklich, still disagree with how the government spends its money: "I'd say the treatment plant and the streets are okay, but they're putting too much money into recreation. Like now they're going to build a big warming house. And it's mostly for the younger people. And like this bus deal they got. The town has a big mill levy every year just to pay for the bus going up to the ski area and back. It benefits the ski area and the businesses, probably, but it doesn't benefit us at all."[9]

Bill Crank says that during the early years of governmental change, he and others in the government were sensitive to the needs of the old-timers and "spent much time trying to devise ways to make it less onerous for them." As a result of the efforts of Crank and others, the old-timers were granted sales tax rebates and sewer and water rebates. If, for example, aside from Social Security, they have an income of less than six thousand dollars a year, they pay less than half what the other townspeople pay for water and trash pick up.[10]

Preparing for paving Elk Avenue, 1980

Despite efforts to make the transition of Crested Butte into a tourist town easier for the old-timers, feelings of hostility and alienation did not wane. Bill Crank says that even though he has amicable relationships with some, he still "... wouldn't suggest that any of the old-timers are close friends of mine." And Rademan remembers most of the discussions he had with them during this period ending in shouting matches. He had some very unpleasant encounters with a few of the less friendly old-timers in town and even received various threats on his life. As a result, he "slept with a gun for five years."11

For a modern government faced with the challenges of a growing tourist industry, the new government of Crested Butte was not attempting to do anything extraordinary. Its increased intervention in the lives of Crested Butte citizens, however, was new and threatening to the old-timers. They felt alienated by those in charge, whom Rademan himself describes as "hippies" who had "all the haughtiness of youth; we really wanted to do something."

Mayor Thom Cox, Joe Sedmak, and Bill Crank, town manager

Moreover, the old-timers felt increasingly displaced in the town that was once their familiar home but was now taking a strange and new direction.[12]

A few old-timers did not feel alienated from the new government, and they actively participated in the change. John Somrak, for example, served on the zoning board for years, which up until the 1970s was dominated by old-timers: "Oh, we shut them guys down. What they didn't try to do, I'll tell you. We shut them down—period." Perhaps because of his outspoken manner, he felt he had a good relationship with the new people and felt free to talk to them: "I used to get along with anybody. The mayor and the town, boy, I used to go up there and argue with them. They used to like that. I used to get along with . . . all them guys, you know." Betty Spehar also became involved with the new government; she has always been active in the Crested Butte Society, which is dedicated to historic preservation, and she also took part in various planning projects in the seventies.[13]

Most of the old-timers, however, did not participate in the local government, a trend that has continued to the present day. They were not as comfortable talking to the new officials as John Somrak was, or perhaps felt their voices would not be heard. Leola Yaklich says about the Crested Butte natives at that time: "We didn't take an active enough part to run our own town."

First sidewalk in Crested Butte on Elk Avenue, 1980

Fred Yaklich disagrees and believes there was nothing the old-timers could have done at the time to influence decision making: "It depends on how many you are. We were outnumbered."[14]

In its efforts to build community spirit in a town made up of disparate elements, the Planning Department stressed the importance of citizen involvement. Its 1973 report described the old-timers as, "except in rare instances, quiet and somewhat unapproachable." The result was that the town residents who responded to the department's efforts to achieve citizen participation were recent arrivals—the "urban refugees." It was a period when the opinions of the old-timers might have been especially valuable because many of the new residents were merely transients who had no real stake in local governmental decisions.[15]

The conflict between the newcomers and those who had lived in Crested Butte all of their lives became more dramatic in 1977–1978. AMAX (formerly

Town meeting, 1983

American Metal Climax, Inc.), the world's largest molybdenum producer, began to implement its plans to mine molybdenum ore at Mt. Emmons, site of the defunct Keystone mine, three miles west of town. A Connecticut-based multinational firm, AMAX had started exploratory drilling in 1974; construction, requiring 2,200 workers, was to start in 1981. The operation of the mine would then begin in 1987, employing 1,450 people, and continue for thirty years. Most of the old-timers were in favor of the project, hoping it would restore mining as the industrial base of the local economy.[16]

The majority of the newer citizens of Crested Butte, including the tourist-oriented business people and W Mitchell, who was town mayor from 1977 to 1981, were opposed to it. A grass-roots interest group, High Country Citizens Alliance (HCCA), was formed in 1977 specifically to fight AMAX. Rademan says that he and others involved in local government at the time saw the AMAX mine as "a huge project that would have eclipsed what we were doing"; it was "the antithesis of what we were working on in Crested Butte."[17]

Mt. Emmons, site of proposed molybdenum mine

The controversy over the AMAX mine showed the old-timers how different their own attitudes and ideas were from those of the new people. The lack of communication and understanding that had typified the relationship between the two groups from the beginning reached a new extreme.

All of the energies of local officials were geared toward fighting the molybdenum mine. Mitchell spent much of his own money flying to Washington to garner support from national politicians. AMAX, for its part, took Mitchell and others on a boom town tour across the West in an effort to prove that the mine would not have disastrous consequences for Crested Butte. The company also made numerous studies to appease fears about the mine, spent $10 million to clean up tailings from the old Keystone Mine, and built a water treatment plant that it still pays $1 million a year to operate.[18]

Despite all of this effort, AMAX left Crested Butte in 1981 because of the collapse in the world molybdenum market. The town ultimately won its case to establish watershed protection in the Colorado Supreme Court, and a watershed district was created around Crested Butte. Previously, Crested Butte controlled only the 217 acres of its original townsite and had no authority over the land outside of town that was to be mined by AMAX. The new Colorado law gave the municipality power to create a district—known as Coal Creek—outside of Crested Butte proper to protect its water supply. The departure of AMAX, seen as a victory by the newcomers of Crested Butte, represented to the old-timers the final, irreversible act of the town being taken away from them.[19]

The AMAX fight was a long, hard struggle that attracted the attention of state-wide and national media. It was an issue that exemplified to many locals and outsiders the increasing tension nationwide between mining interests and the preservation of local environments. Arthur Townsend, state historical preservation officer, was quoted in *The Denver Post* as saying about the issue:

Protesting against the AMAX mine

It is so complex and includes so many currently significant issues in the nation today. There's the historical value, the potential archaeological, recreational, wilderness, economic values, a tremendous resource and mining potential. It's all there, and it challenges the way the country traditionally makes decisions. Do we really need molybdenum so much that we must allow degradation of this historic town and its natural environment?[20]

By 1979, the newcomers in Crested Butte had tripled the population of 1970, and lots that had sold for $15 just after the mines closed were selling for $25 thousand. Crested Butte was no longer a workingman's town, and its new residents were determined to protect what they had come to enjoy. Bruce Baumgartner, who became Crested Butte's first town manager, said at the time: "The real issue is whether a tourist-based economy can coexist with a mine without damaging the environment. The majority of the people here left the cities and high-paying jobs and are pretty protective about their lifestyle."[21]

The Mt. Emmons project would have been very different from the coal mining that had gone on in Crested Butte. In the mining of molybdenum, 99.6 percent of the rock taken out of the mountain is useless and must be disposed of elsewhere. Opponents of the mine on Mt. Emmons pointed to AMAX's Climax Mine outside of Leadville,

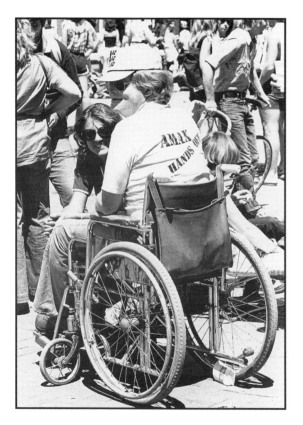

W Mitchell, mayor of Crested Butte, leader of the opposition to AMAX

Colorado, which had been in operation since 1917, as an example of what would happen to Crested Butte. Around the collapsed Bartlett Mountain south of Leadville, miles of valley are filled with tailings from the mine. In addition to the environmental devastation, people were also concerned about the social implications of creating a possible boom town situation. Crested Butte's population was expected to increase by as many as 13 thousand people by 1986, when the mine was to be in full operation. Finally, there was the economic argument against the mine, which, as Mitchell says, was "as much cosmetic as anything," since "Who wants to ski in a boom town?"[22]

Most of the old-timers had a very different perspective from the newcomers and could not understand why anyone would want to prevent a stable industry from returning to Crested Butte—especially the mining industry. John Somrak used to argue with the local leadership: "I told them, Mitch and those guys—the mayor—'What the hell you guys fighting mining for? You know something, mining made Crested Butte. Mining made Colorado! If it wasn't for mining, there would be no Crested Butte, and you suckers wouldn't be here either.'"[23]

Most old-timers, like Lyle McNeill, felt that AMAX would have done good things for the town, and that a valuable opportunity was lost when the company left:

> AMAX was good, because humanity has got to depend on progress and without it you don't have very much . . . the thing that happened with AMAX was the town council up here was so scared that AMAX was going to move in that they turned down a lot of things worth an awful lot of money . . . they didn't have sense enough . . . their main thoughts behind it were, well, AMAX is going to take over the town, going to run it. And the City Council wanted to run it themselves. But they turned down some of the greatest things that could ever have happened to a community.

Congressman John Seiberling, David Brower of the Sierra Club, and Tom Nelson of the U.S. Forest Service offer Mayor W Mitchell their support, 1980.

Teeny Tezak also saw the controversy as an example of how the new people did not know what was good for the town; to him, the decision to fight AMAX was incomprehensible: "They don't reason things, that's the problem. They don't reason what's better. If they'd have let AMAX alone, all that money they invested in the streets, improvements, sewer lines, water lines, AMAX would have done all of that for them, just like they did in Buena Vista and Leadville."[24]

Old-timers like Johnny Krizmanich saw molybdenum mining not only as a financial benefit to the town, but as a means of returning to a more stable and more familiar form of existence: "That would have been a good thing for Crested Butte. Leadville's got AMAX there. They've done everything they possibly could for that town. And miners are good people.

They're hard-working people. They don't bother you near as much as the element you got up there now." Betty Spehar agrees that the return of a major industry would have benefited the community overall: "I would rather see Crested Butte as a working-person's town than a pure tourist town myself. Real families, stable families. Not so much transiency as you now have. A lot more stability, better schools, you know, in general. It would be a much more stable community than it is."[25]

Many of the old-timers saw local opposition as another illustration of the newcomers' selfish desire to determine the future direction of the town. Joe Sedmak and others feel that their insensitivity was the result of their having outside means of income, which prevented them from understanding the needs of working people:

> They just wanted to make more of a recreation town. And they want to keep a nice haven all to themselves. They probably figured they were better. I think that was the case with old Mitchell at that time, he had a lot of money, he thought he could run the town. If they'd let the mining come, this town would be a better town today.[26]

Those who had spent much of their lives in or around coal mines did not see how the AMAX mine could cause any more environmental damage than the Big Mine had in its fifty-year existence. They did not understand the environmentalist point of view. As Teeny Tezak said, "You take that Gibson Ridge. There's been millions and millions of tons of coal taken out of there, and it's still holding its same shape." Fred Yaklich was also in favor of the mine and never believed the environmental protest that it would cause all of Mt. Emmons to cave in: "Oh, I don't think it'd ever cave in. There's always a way to do things right. I've got a feeling like this: as long as he does it right, he ought to be able to do it."[27]

Many others felt the environmental costs could not outweigh the benefits of the mine. A popular refrain among old-timers about the scenery around Crested Butte was that yes, it is a beautiful place, but "you can't eat scenery." They believed there needed to be an industry that produced something more tangible than a beautiful view and provided more steady wages. Tony Stefanic expresses his reservations about environmentalists:

> These environment people, what are you going to do? One lady was complaining about environment this, environment that. I said "Lady, I'll give you a question. You give me an answer, will you? Now I got this piece of bread here. Can you go up there and get some of that green tree or branches or whatever and put it together and make a sandwich?" "Well, I guess not." I says, "Where are you going to get it from?"[28]

Not all of the old-timers felt the same way about AMAX. Leola Yaklich, for example, agreed with the environmentalists at that time: "I was diametrically opposed to AMAX because they were going to strip mine . . . to me, it was great to see that a small community could go up against a big industrial giant and push them back and that's just what happened."

Many of the old-timers did not believe the environmental damage could be so serious. Molybdenum mining was very different from what they knew and its effects on the environment were significantly more damaging than those caused by the coal mines of their day. As a result, says Leola Yaklich, "They didn't really understand." But even Fred Yaklich, who supported AMAX, adds that he would not be in favor of that kind of destruction of the mountain: "No, to mine it that way, I wouldn't be for that."[29]

The AMAX controversy became especially bitter when it was evident that many of the local residents were as concerned about having an increased population of miners as they were about the destruction of Mt. Emmons. Some pointed to boom strip-mining towns like Craig, Colorado, and Gillette, Wyoming, where there was rampant alcoholism, crime, and even prostitution, as examples of what would happen to Crested Butte. Opponents of AMAX employed the "stability" argument. Mitchell was most concerned about the first phase of construction and says that "the transitory nature of it" was "horrifying." Teachers would have had a complete turnover in students within a single year. Overall, says Mitchell, the transiency of the project would have discouraged the formation of stable values and attitudes and therefore would have been very destructive of the community. The fact is, Mitchell claims, skiers as a whole are better educated than miners and they bring their money to a community, enjoy themselves, and then go home. There are far fewer social problems and much lower crime rates in places like Crested Butte, Vail, and Aspen than there are in boom towns like Craig and Rock Springs.³⁰

Parade car protest, Fourth of July, 1981

Concerns about rapid growth were valid, but many of the arguments included insensitive, derogatory generalizations about miners, which offended Crested Butte natives. Johnny Krizmanich and others were convinced that the new people harbored elitist attitudes: "In my mind, it's that these skiers thought they were so much better than the miners who were working up there at the time. That's where they got the idea that miners are no good. But they are." Gwen Danni remembers the editorials that were in the paper at the time about how Crested Butte did not want more miners:

> I think the thing that made us most angry—of course we both had miners as ancestors—was when it came out in the controversy how the miners were no good, and they wouldn't let their children go to school with the miners' children. I mean they were being that extreme. And when you get your extremists like that, that's when we began to think, "Well, just who do you think you are? Because drugs came in with your ski thing, you brought a whole different set of problems." So we would rather have the hard-working class.[31]

The newcomers' prejudices reminded Joe Saya of the college kids in Gunnison who, when the coal mines were operating, would get into fights with miners at local dances: "They think the miners are deadbeats. It's just like them kids when they were up in Gunnison going to college . . . and miners are the ones that built this town." Betty Spchar also says that the new people's attitude was "Keep the miners out" and believes they did not realize that their arguments would offend local old-timers who had needed to make a living by mining: "See, they were not sensible or rational. Or they were spoiled enough not to realize what it was like to have to make a living when there was no government support that you could turn to, there was no Social Security or handicap, or anything like that."[32]

Mitchell perceived the situation, again, as the clash between two different attitudes and ways of life. He was aware of the hostility many of the old-timers felt toward him because of what he represented in their eyes: "I was the guy running the town and the guy against mining. I have no doubt we said all kinds of things that could easily have been interpreted as affronts." Rademan agrees that the anti-AMAX arguments "started to denigrate everything about mining and that invalidated their whole lives." Perhaps Mitchell sums up the entire conflict and breach of understanding between the old-timers and newcomers in saying: "All they saw was us rallying against mining, against progress, against all their old friends. They saw Crested Butte returning to the good old days and all we saw was Gillette, Wyoming."[33]

The old-timers were most disturbed by the newcomers' extremism and irrational inconsistency. As Joe Danni observes, "The most radical ones didn't understand what was really going on. They're the same kind that don't want you to cut a tree because it'll ruin the forest and the same kind that don't want a cow in the hills—you know, they got their own view and that's it."[34]

Johnny Krizmanich argues that the town's decision to turn toward tourism and development rather than industry has led to greater ecological damage than the AMAX mine ever would have done: "Mining does not ruin the mountain. One year when we were coming back from a trip, we flew over Crested Butte Mountain, and it was disgusting to see. Just the way they chopped it up. And miners . . . never do that." Betty Spehar makes a similar observation: "Did they yell when Crested Butte Mountain was so defaced? For the ski trails? And did they object to the wonderful lightweight bicycle frames that they were all crazy about using, for which molybdenum was a key element? No."[35]

Despite their stated reverence for the old-timers of Crested Butte, the young newcomers running the town were determined to fight AMAX, whatever the cost. They saw Crested Butte in symbolic terms as one of the last great havens in this country that needed to be saved from the onslaught of exploitative industry, which was notorious for destroying so much of the American West. In Mitchell's words, Crested Butte was not just a home, but "a phenomenal resource" and "magnificent place where you can live on the edge of the wilderness." And AMAX embodied all of the evils of industry as a company that, as Mitchell says, "had all the money in the world and had never been told 'no' before."[36]

By winning their fight against AMAX, the newcomers succeeded in protecting what they had come to Crested Butte to enjoy: pristine wilderness and an alternative way of life removed from the unpleasantness of modern society. And in preserving their vision of Crested Butte, they permanently eradicated the old-timers' hopes that Crested Butte would be a mining town once again.

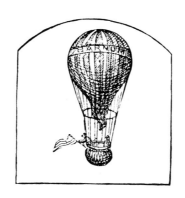

RECREATION, FESTIVALS, TOURISTS

What would the first men and women who struggled to make a living in the days of coal think of today's Crested Butte? Teeny Tezak does not think his parents would like what they saw: "I believe they'd think it's lousy. Because the people are mostly loafing around. It's a different method of life, is all." Joe Sedmak thinks his father would not believe the way people are living: "I don't know . . . my dad would just shake his head. In his time when they started paying unemployment, twenty dollars a week, he couldn't believe they would give you money for nothing. They were used to work and they didn't get something for nothing." Tony Stefanic believes his parents would react more vehemently: "They'd flip in their grave. They'd look at this and say, 'I think I want to go back where I came from. I don't want no part of what's going on now.'"[1]

The old-timers agree that some change in Crested Butte was inevitable. There was no possible economic base for the town but tourism and, even if the coal mines had stayed open, the community would not be the same. Most of the children of the old-timers would still have moved away to go to college or to work elsewhere; few would have gone into mining. Many old-timers had different ambitions for their children than they did for themselves. Joe Saya speaks with pride of his children's accomplishments: "No, they wouldn't be here because I know my kids; I'd have sent them through college and they'd have went out to work some place else. Two sons and a daughter, they went to college and they're all doing good." Even people of Betty Spehar's generation, ten years younger than most of the old-timers, were already moving away from Crested Butte when the mines were still in operation, getting college degrees and becoming lawyers, doctors, and professors.[2]

Racers line up on Elk Avenue during Fat Bike Tire Week, 1990

Despite the inevitability of the change, however, many of the old-timers naturally lament what has been lost. Joe Saya put it simply: "I liked it better then than I do now. I think in them days people helped one another, they were more friendly and everything else. The generation now, it seems they've changed altogether different." The rapid turnover in population makes it difficult to get to know people: "Well, it's changing every year; different people come in here, like ten, fifteen years ago, buy and start a business, and they'd sell it to somebody else maybe two, three years, and then somebody else. Like I said, there's nobody I know up there anymore. I can go up and down that street there and I wouldn't know nobody." Josephine Stajduhar expresses her love for the way Crested Butte was and contrasts it with the change that she feels has robbed the town of the joy it once provided:

Oooh, it was wonderful. My God, it was wonderful. That's why I said, I don't enjoy being outside, or nothing. I'd rather sit in the house working my puzzles. I don't know these people, and the only time I get out in the front is when I sprinkle the front yard. Like I said, it isn't home. When we talk to people when they come, I say "Where's the happiness?" There's no happiness no more. There's no happiness. That's how I feel.[3]

Johnny Krizmanich also expresses a sense of alienation: "I can pick up the paper right there, and I read it and I won't see two people that I know . . . It didn't used to be that way. Used to know everybody." Johnny feels like an outsider in his own town, a stranger in the place that to him was so special because of its size and intimacy. Asked how it feels not to know people anymore, he said:

Crested Butte claims to be mountain bike capital of the world.

Well, it don't make you happy. You have people lived in Crested Butte and they come back and look around and say, "What did these people do to our town?" It just isn't Crested Butte. Changed too drastically. People . . . people make a place change, it doesn't just change itself. The whole town just changed, that's all.[4]

Other old-timers are less disturbed by the changes. While they recognize differences between themselves and the new people and agree that the community is permanently altered, they are more acceptant. Teeny Tezak, for example, explains that he was not as affected as others by the various developments: "Oh, I didn't pay any attention to it. I had all kinds of work." Asked how he feels about the change, John Somrak responds: "It's good. I like it, it suits me. Had to be something, couldn't be the way it was."5

Lyle McNeill continues to see the change in terms of progress, which he equates to economic growth and financial gain. He does not lament the loss of community, ". . . because without a change in your lifestyle and your home and the environment around it, it isn't very long until you're going to lose everything." And Tony Mihelich, while recognizing the vast differences between the way Crested Butte was and the way it is today, has positive things to say about the new people: "I find them all to be honest and good." About the younger people who run the town government, he adds: "They're better educated today. Some have very progressive ideas and know what's best for the town."6

Extreme skiing and hot dogging, as well as cross-country and telemark skiing, are now Crested Butte trademarks.

The old-timers differ in how they feel about what has happened in Crested Butte in the past forty years, but nearly all of them marvel at the dramatic changes that have taken place. Today, Crested Butte enjoys growing popularity as a ski resort that offers challenging slopes to expert skiers. It also attracts more and more visitors every summer with its growing number of summertime activities, including an array of concerts and dance recitals, Fat Tire Bike Week, Wildflower Festival, Aerial Weekend, and Arts Fair. Crested Butte is by some accounts the mountain-bike capital of the world, and even has a Mountain Bike Hall of Fame that traces the evolution of the one gear klunker into the twenty-four speed mountain bike.

An increasing number of tourists come to town for the Fourth of July every summer to watch the now-famous annual Crested Butte Fourth of July parade on Elk Avenue. The parade is known for its small-town originality and includes an eclectic mixture of floats—from polka musicians and dancers to a snowmobile set atop a mound of real snow brought down from the high country—as well as local ranchers and outfitters on horseback. Then there are the scientists and students from the Rocky Mountain Biological Laboratory located in the nearby town of Gothic, who dance down the street clad in skunk cabbage skirts to the noisy rhythm of whistles, pots, and pans. Eager parade watchers need not be concerned if they miss part of the procession, since the parade always turns around to march the route a second time, in the opposite direction.

Arts Fair, 1990

This new Eden of mountain bikes, arts festivals, and skiing has taken over the world of the old-timers. But like the Crested Butte of that era, the town is still small, and relatively remote, and those of the younger generation feel they know each other. The balance between the town's amenities and its population is presently a good one. For this reason, there is anxiety and apprehension about what lies ahead.

The rapid pace of change that threatens to erase the past, and alter the present beyond recognition as well, is part of a larger pattern happening all over the West. Because of the increasing number of people who want to be able to escape from urban areas, population pressures are growing and land values are rising. The result is that people who have traditionally made their living from the land are being pushed out. The entire Gunnison Valley is going the way of Crested Butte, turning to tourism and development. The same environmentalists who condemned the ranchers, and the lovers of the out-of-doors who cursed at cows and overgrazed areas, are now witnessing the subdivision and development of the wide open spaces that served as ranchland and made the valley beautiful.

The ranchers, like the coal miners, had established strong communities where they settled. And they, too, have watched their communities all but disappear. Joe Danni was born and raised on the ranch that his father started in the early part of the century. He echoes statements of Johnny Krizmanich in saying that ranching is "all I know."

Balloon ascension during Aerial Weekend

Joe grew up when there was a community of twenty ranching families in the valley from the town of Almont to Crested Butte and all the children went to school at the local one-room schoolhouse. He remembers social gatherings when the families got together to help each other brand and ship their cattle out to Denver and Kansas City and to share Thanksgiving dinners. By the time he and his wife Gwen were married, the traditional way of ranch life was little more than a memory. Today, there are only four ranch families left in the area.[7]

Cattle drive from summer grazing in
Washington Gulch to ranches down valley

Dora Mae Trampe's father-in-law rode the train from Illinois to the town of Salida, Colorado, at the turn of the century and came over Monarch Pass (the second highest mountain pass in Colorado) on a bicycle. He eventually became one of the biggest ranchers in the area. Before Dora Mae married into the family in 1945, there were eleven or twelve ranchers that ran cattle together. The roundup crew was always made up of men from the various ranches. Today, there is no shared range area, and no more roundup crews; each ranch has its own allotment and operates independently.[8]

As it becomes increasingly difficult to make a living, more and more ranchers are selling their land to developers and moving away. With land values going up and property taxes escalating, there is little incentive for them to stay. Dora Mae explains the pattern of what is happening in the valley: "A lot of our property, we're in a prime recreational area. If there's a place for sale, there's always some recreational guy or moneyed man who wants to make a playground out of it. You can't blame people for selling it that way and that's what's happening." She believes the change is as inevitable in the valley as it was in Crested Butte: "We're going to turn into a recreational area, there's just no doubt about it."[9]

The Dannis have already sold some land, and "The Danni Ranch" is a major new development just south of Crested Butte. As Gwen says, "We're right in the midst of it, too, because we have sold. And it just broke our heart, but what are we going to do? Our sons couldn't make a living off of it, it's too small. . . ."[10]

Ranching in the valley, like mining in Crested Butte, was fundamental to the economy of the area not long ago, but the community that once existed as the Dannis describe it is gone. With the advent of tourism and recreation, and more people wanting to use the valley as a vacation spot, ranching as a way of life has nearly disappeared.

V

THE CHALLENGES

Y ou really can't control the tourism or the rapid development. This summer is the first time I've really felt that it's going to be too much. Thank God we're as isolated as we are and difficult to get to. And so we've never had anything like a rapid boom. If we become, you know, a prized tourist spot, where the billionaires replace the millionaires, it's going to be an artificial place, like Aspen and Vail. And you're going to lose the good families and all of that. And I think it has been happening, just progressing more slowly. I'm afraid that we can't avoid it. Given the nature of modern communication, transportation, and the fact that it is so stunningly, gloriously beautiful.[1]

Betty Spehar

While Crested Butte, like the valley, has changed, its physical isolation so far has protected it from the condominium and strip shopping center development that characterizes many Colorado recreation areas. There is still a strong community in Crested Butte today. Although a large part of the population continues to be transient, there are a number of hard-working inhabitants who have been settled here for ten or twenty years. These are the people who are raising the new generation of Crested Butte natives and are

A long tradition of community celebration, Memorial Day, 1983

dedicated to building their community and preserving their way of life.

Many of these newer citizens came to town to ski, but rather than move on after a ski season or two they made Crested Butte their home. George Sibley, writer and now coordinator of special projects and professor of journalism at Western State College in Gunnison, arrived in Crested Butte in 1966 after reading in the paper in Denver that the ski area, although bankrupt, would still be open for the winter. Glo Cunningham, who is involved in just about every community activity in town, came in 1975, having just returned from a five-year trip around the world, after which she decided that she could not face living in mainstream America. Thom Cox, former mayor and president of the Crested Butte Bank, has been in Crested Butte for twenty three years. He left Wichita, Kansas, where he worked for a large bank, and when he first came to Crested Butte he worked as a carpenter, drove the bus up to the ski area, and waited tables two nights a week.[2]

Jim Schmidt rode into town on his motorcycle in the summer of 1976 while on a bicentennial tour of the country, and never left. Sandy Fails, local author and writer for the *Crested Butte Chronicle* and *The Crested Butte Magazine*, came in 1981 and at the time "had no sense that I was moving here for the rest of my life." And Gary Sprung, president of High Country Citizens Alliance, arrived in 1979, because, as he says, he was looking for "a place where I could cross-country ski out my backyard, where there were interesting environmental politics, and where there was a real community. Crested Butte was the only place that offered those three things." Sandy might speak for all of these citizens of Crested Butte who came to ski and stayed, when she says: "I may have moved here as a ski bum, but I have a deep stake in this town now."[3]

Memorial Day, 1983

There is also a small group of Crested Butte natives who grew up here in the 1950s and 1960s and still live in town. Gary Sporcich, who is Tony Mihelich's grandson, says a lot of his relatives did not understand why he came back after going to college on the East Coast. He returned simply because "it felt like this was where I wanted to be." In addition, he says, after growing up in the years when many people were wondering whether the town was going to survive, Crested Butte had suddenly become a magnet: "I was drawn to the energy of the young people coming to town. It was a group that thought they were the pioneers of something new and different. I realized that those coming were saying this was the future."[4]

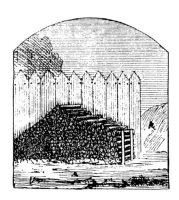

While there were clashes in lifestyle and disagreements between the old-timers and the new people over how the town should be run, there were also opportunities for the different generations to get to know one another and build special friendships. Glo Cunningham describes the polkas, the barbecues, and yard parties where the old-timers and the new people came together. Birthdays were important events, often with traditional pig roasts; and Memorial Day was a special day honored by all in town.[5]

Some of the recent arrivals took special interest in learning about the history of the town through the old-timers. Sandra Cortner began to chronicle their lives in the late 1960s through her photography and interviews. Working for the paper gave Sandy Fails the excuse to conduct a series of interviews as well. She says it was the old-timers that drew her most to Crested Butte: "Instantly, I just had this feeling . . . there was something about this place that really fascinated me."[6]

Gary Sporcich remembers the old-timers as having a significant influence on the new arrivals: "The people moving in were assuming some of the values that were here before. They were very impressed by the old lifestyles and values. Being accepted by the old-timers was a big thing."[7]

The presence of the old-timers gave the town a living history and many of the newcomers developed a feeling of connection to it. Sandy Fails says: "Early on, it gave me a sense of the roots of the town, a dimension that makes it so much richer. It makes you realize that you are part of a continuum . . . We are part of a progression of things. It's not as if the town had a history that stopped at one point, and now we've entered a totally different stage. History is still happening here." She adds that when people feel this and understand it, they become more careful of preserving the town's uniqueness: "If you view Crested Butte as a ski resort, it can be just another generic ski resort. But if you get to know the town, and understand its roots, it becomes a special place on the earth, and you naturally feel more of a stake in it. The town has a different richness."[8]

"Being accepted by the old-timers was a big thing."

Committed to the place in which they landed, the new people built on the tradition of community that had been established by the old-timers, whom George Sibley remembers as being "very close, like an extended clan." George adds: "It was a group of people taking care of a town, and thereby taking care of each other." The newcomers, too, were committed to making the town a warm, welcoming place where they could depend on each other for assistance and friendship. It is a tradition that has been carried on into the present day, and people in Crested Butte speak proudly of their community and their involvement in it.[9]

One resident who exemplifies this pattern, having spent the last twenty years getting involved in, or even running, most community events that have taken place, is Glo Cunningham. Her activities have included serving three years on the Board of Directors of the Mountain Theater, performing in nine plays, running the Summit Telemark Series for seven years, running the North American Telemark Championships, volunteering at Fat Tire Bike Week for several years, regularly attending Town Council meetings, and serving on the board of the Land Trust. As Glo says, "One of the brilliant things about Crested Butte is you can do anything you want to do. For example, I was a radio DJ for four years. Where else could I have done something like that? You can realize so many goals here." She has also gotten into the habit of going to the post office every year during the last two days of voter registration and reminding people to register.[10]

Generations mix at Flaushink, celebration of Spring—John Somrak, festival queen Sherry Vandervoort, Lyle McNeill, and festival king Bill Crank, Crested Butte Town Manager

There are many residents who devote time and energy to various community activities and institutions, such as the local schools, the volunteer fire department, the volunteer Emergency Medical Technicians (EMTs), the various summer festivals and, of course, the softball teams. Glo Cunningham says the community in Crested Butte is "phenomenal."[207] Jim Schmidt feels the same way: "Everybody talks about their community and people are always proud of their communities, which is great. But inside I always chuckle and laugh at them and think, well, we have the real community here." Sandy Fails agrees that Crested Butte has something different: "To me, it's the human community that is the heart and soul of this place." It is a place, says Sandy, that "invites out the best in people." She adds, "There's a very steady stream of giving to this community. I think the more you give to a place, the more loyal you become. People that give the most to a community are the people that get the most from it."[12]

The town pulls together in times of tragedy, as well as during periods of well-being. When the Crested Butte bank exploded in March of 1990, the

The Ruthless Babes win the softball championship, 1979

town responded immediately to the trauma. Three women — two mothers—were killed in the blast, and the tragedy deeply affected everybody. As Sandy says, during times of misfortune "the town is just there." She adds that, while in cities it is easy to remain anonymous and not look out for others, "here, there's an implied responsibility for each other's well-being."[13]

The people who settled in Crested Butte during the interim years have seen a lot of changes from the small, remote, nearly forgotten place it was when they arrived. Their descriptions of how the town has changed echo the old-timers' stories. During the first winter that George Sibley was in Crested Butte, he worked as a ski patrolman. He says that in January there were often days when the seven on-duty members of the ski patrol outnumbered the paying skiers on the mountain. According to George, people could also rent houses at the time for $90 a month during the winter, and the Academy Arms, now the Forest Queen, rented rooms for $35 a month.[14]

Today, such stories sound like fables. Despite the dramatic changes that have occurred, however, the basic issues of the town remain the same. George bought the *Crested Butte Chronicle* in 1968 for one dollar and a six-month printing contract. Even back then, says George, most of the stories were about growth and affordable housing and everyone was saying, "We don't want to become another Aspen." The April 22, 1970, issue had two major headlines: Earth Day and the sale of the ski area to Bo Callaway. As George points out, the two stories symbolize the ongoing tension between the two identities of the town: a small community where people cherish their way of life and want to protect both their community and the larger natural environment, and a ski town that is seeking to draw ever-greater numbers of tourists and that measures its value by the pace of development and the amount of cash that exchanges hands.[15]

What exists now in Crested Butte is something of a blend of these two identities, creating a balance which many of the townspeople consciously work to maintain. They view the recent surge of interest in the town and surrounding valleys with great apprehension.

Perhaps the most threatening intrusion is the unprecedented amount of outside money coming into the area. A new breed of speculators has arrived in Crested Butte to make their fortunes, not dissimilar in their goals from the early gold and silver miners who invaded the Gunnison area in the 1870s. Jim Schmidt says these speculators are to be distinguished from the people who have been coming to Crested Butte for the past twenty five years: "There have always been those who wanted to make money, but most were here because they really loved the place. Now there are people coming just to make a killing . . . there's opportunity for people like that." Gary Sporcich adds: "A lot of people today don't come to Crested Butte because they see here's this great community and say 'I want to be a part of it.' People now are seeing investment opportunities, and what then happens is it becomes like any other place."[16]

Gary Sprung agrees that the phenomenon of people coming just to make money is a threat to the community: "Most people move here for an alternative lifestyle, not to get rich. They want a close relationship with nature, good recreation, and arts. Growth does not serve their interests. Aspenization is the great fear. But in the past five years, we've actually seen people moving here to get rich quick. They are the new greatest threat. They are the new AMAX. They are a threat to the values that people came here for."[17]

Crested Butte, 1966. The appearance of the town is altered as older, smaller buildings are replaced by newer, larger ones. These lots along Coal Creek have since been developed.

A lot of Crested Butte residents say they are not opposed to new people in general—just the ones that come for purely selfish, exploitative reasons. As Jim Schmidt says, "I've never questioned anybody who moved here and said, 'It's a beautiful place. I really like it.' But I would question someone who said 'I want to make a lot of money here,' or had the attitude, 'I want to take out of this town, and not give to it.'" Glo Cunningham is also opposed to people coming to town for what she considers to be the wrong reasons: "I can't say I don't want more people coming to town because I came to town, too, and was very welcome." However, she adds: "Nobody should be coming here for big bucks."[18]

The infusion of so much outside money drives up expenses, while wages fail to rise commensurately. One of the results is that people are forced to work more jobs, and they have less time to become involved in the community and to enjoy the quality of life for which they moved to Crested Butte in the first place. The more dramatic effect of rising prices is that hard-working people are forced to leave because they cannot afford to live in Crested Butte anymore.

Mothers and daughters celebrate Vintok Harvest Festival, 1993, which features cross-generational storytelling, a community potluck, and polka dancing.

Sandy Fails points out that it is becoming increasingly difficult to make "the leap from ski bum to a settled-in person who wants to make a life here." She explains that people who move to Crested Butte in their twenties can live six people to a house because it's "part of the experience." But they reach the stage when they want a different kind of life: "When you put down roots, you want more of a sense of permanence." People who cannot afford to move out of the shared house might leave town rather than becoming long-term, contributing members of its community. Jim Schmidt feels the most pressing need is to "keep the people here who are vital—the volunteers who serve as EMTs and participate in the Mountain Theater, the DJs on the radio . . . the people who are the heart and soul of the town."[19]

The most visible result of more money coming into the area is the growth in housing developments. Many of the subdivisions that were approved and planned years ago are now being built. New houses are constantly under construction, some in town but mostly on parcels of surrounding land that were once ranch properties. Increasingly, trails that people have been accustomed to hiking and biking on for years are being fenced off or bulldozed over into

Elk Avenue, 1995 — Traffic and parking regulations, but as yet, no stoplights or meters

driveways and roads, and more and more of the views from town are of large new homes rather than pristine mountainsides.

Some of the effects of development and growth are more subtle. The influence of new money and the arrival of so many new people give many of the current residents a sense of alienation they never felt before. Sandy says it is not unlike what the old-timers experienced in the 1960s: "The people who came here in the past ten, twenty years, their kids are natives of Crested Butte and I think we feel invaded, to a certain degree, like the old-timers did." Town Manager Bill Crank tells the story of recently going for dinner to a local restaurant, where the prices have gotten so expensive since he moved to town in the early 1970s that he can only afford to eat there a few times a year. The reaction he had upon walking in the door echoes the feelings of so many of the old-timers: "I didn't know anybody else in the restaurant. For the first time, I had the fringe feeling of disenfranchisement."[20]

Gary Sporcich says the loss of space where people can casually socialize has been gradual, but has had an impact on community life: "Recently, they've turned over a lot of the key areas of town, like Elk Avenue, to tourism and outsiders. This has tended to push the community farther away. Noon at the post office always used to be a community event, up until five years ago. That's no longer the case." Gary thinks the post office itself, which has long been a place where people congregate during the day, will soon have to be moved out of the center of town because it's beginning to create too much traffic where it is. He adds: "It's not just the growth, it's the activity. There's just more buzz, gridlock, commotion, commerce. This affects the way people interact."[21]

The level of community involvement is changing as well. There is still a strong tradition of participation in town life but, as Sandy Fails observes, "There's less of that now, less of the sense of getting involved and giving back to the community." She adds: "I still see an extremely strong community here, but it is different, and it is changing." George Sibley shares the fears of others and believes the greatest threat facing the town is "a declining sense of that community where we all take care of the place, and in the process the place and we take care of each other . . . something that no matter how much money you have, you can't buy."[22]

The citizens of Crested Butte differ in where they think the town should go. Most are still extremely wary of growth, while others lean toward increased growth and development. George Sibley expresses the practical view that people must be realistic about what is happening and warns that being antigrowth can prevent people from seeing and addressing the challenges around them: "There is a tendency to come here and say 'this place is great, it's perfect, we don't want to change a thing.' This, I think, becomes a very destructive tendency because it indicates no understanding of how nature and culture work." He adds that the people of Crested Butte should focus on those issues over which they can exercise some control: "We can't stop all of these things. The question is how to put together a package that works best for us and makes it as difficult as possible for those things we don't want to happen. You have to do what you can locally to accommodate those things you can't change, and change the things you can." Gary Sporcich expresses a similar view: "A major concern is whether we'll be able to stop debating whether there will be change—because there will be—and come to terms with how that change is implemented."[23]

One of the most talked-about issues is the possible expansion of the ski area onto Snodgrass Mountain. Those who support the expansion, like Thom Cox, think that the opposition should be more realistic and willing to discuss the different options: "If we sat down, we could work out some reasonable compromise." Thom adds that there needs to be some development in order for the town to thrive: "We have to have some growth, or we're going to go backwards. This whole place is built on recreation. But we need to do it in a responsible way, and I think we can." George Sibley is opposed to the expansion, but says he would prefer to spend his time and energy making sure that the ski area pays its way. He agrees with Thom that any development should be done responsibly and says there should be more negotiation so that any expansion provides affordable housing and other benefits he believes would help stabilize the local community.[24]

The Knights of Pythia lodge, transformed, 1995

There are others who think the ski area expansion will only speed up the growth that is already occurring. Jim Schmidt fears that this acceleration will undermine the quality of life in Crested Butte: "The problem with ski area expansion is that it demands that growth occur so much more rapidly. It becomes like a boom town and the infrastructure then can't keep up with the growth." It is not a question of wanting to stop growth altogether, says Jim, but of wanting it to be more measured: "We're going to grow anyhow, but if they double the size of the ski area, they'll have to get more people in here to pay for it."[25]

Gary Sprung believes that whether Snodgrass is developed is the bellwether issue that will determine the future of the town and of the valley: "We're at a crossroads. If we succeed in halting and significantly delaying Snodgrass, we might actually be able to put some sanity into development in Crested Butte." In response to the notion that eventual ski area development is going to happen despite the level of opposition, Sprung says: "That's exactly what they said about AMAX, that AMAX was inevitable and we should compromise."[26]

With the ski area expansion, and the ongoing debates over a multitude of issues, many agree with Gary Sprung that Crested Butte is "at a crossroads." No one can predict what the future will bring. The old-timers have their own differences of opinion. Lyle McNeill, in celebrating the growth, foresees a bright future for the town as a prime tourist area. When asked what he feels is so special about Crested Butte, he describes the opportunity to

1994 attendees at the Red Lady Ball held yearly to raise funds for the High Country Citizen's Alliance. "The Red Lady" is an affectionate name for Mt. Emmons, site of the defeated AMAX molybdenum mine. Gary Sprung, president of HCCA, is in the back row.

Ski area, 1995

benefit financially from the beautiful scenery that abounds:

> Well, a lot of things are special about Crested Butte. But I'm going to tell you one thing. I have predicted for several years now that from Almont up to Crested Butte, in a few years' time, is going to become one of the biggest tourist places in the state of Colorado. Due to the openness of the valley, the fishing, the ski area, and everything like that—I don't know if I'm right or wrong, but that's my prediction.[27]

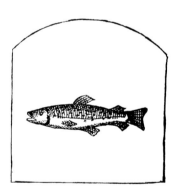

Most old-timers, however, express misgivings and fear about further development. Tony Mihelich is content with the way Crested Butte is today:

"All these people moving in, making it their home, it's a good place to live. It's not yet too big." He then carefully adds: "But if it keeps growing the way it is, it might be. I wouldn't like to see it get too big like Aspen and Vail. You never know what's going to happen." Teeny Tezak suspects that the town is not careful enough about growth: "That's the trouble, there's no regulations. Or there are regulations, but they're not enforced. If they're not enforced, they don't mean nothing." And Johnny Krizmanich believes that Crested Butte will continue to be changed at the cost of the community:

1995 Flaushink Festival affords opportunity to protest development of Snodgrass Mountain

> These people are getting too many big-town ideas for a small town. They say they didn't want to be like Aspen, they don't want to be like that place, but they do, 'cause they're doing it, see. We used to go to council meetings once in a while, they say, "We don't want this place to get like Aspen." It is that way now. Hell, maybe it could get better. It couldn't get a hell of a lot worse, could it? It couldn't get much worse than it is right now.[28]

Joe Saya shares the fear that the town will eventually "become just another glitzy ski resort" and undermines the stereotype of the anti-environmental miner saying: "Development is ruining this nice mountain country now. I don't like it. I like it better when you see the nice scenery, the mountains and everything else. And the developers will come in and build all over."[29]

Leola Yaklich puts it simply: "I guess we're changing from a rural atmosphere to an urban atmosphere." And she worries that the future of Crested Butte lies in the hands of the privileged few: "I'm very disturbed because I feel it's going to be the wealthy. And all they make of the rest of us is 'their peons.' Not all of them. There are nice wealthy people. But as a rule, they want to run everything and control wherever they are. And that's what I object to. For example, the rich are buying up all the property around here."[30]

Many of the newer residents share the old-timers' fears for the future and wonder how much can be controlled. As Jim Schmidt says, "Growth is certainly the issue, and the issue that has no answer. If half of California thinks this is a great place to move to, there isn't a whole lot we can do. And on top of this, there are the new speculators in town, which makes things crazy."

Four generations in Crested Butte. Sisters Mildred McNeill and Vonda Rozman (*back*) Joyce Rozman Cobai, daughter Melina, and Matriarch Jessie Richardson (*front*).

John Hess, town planner, foresees that growth will continue to be gradual, "unless we get 'discovered.'" John previously worked in Routt County where Steamboat Springs is located, and also for a Council of Governments which included Aspen, Vail, and other large ski areas. About these ski towns, he says: "They all have the same problems." Jim agrees: "It's the path everybody's headed down. Aspen is at one end, and Grand Lake on the other. We're somewhere in between." John says he "tries not to have a vision" for the future, and adds: "The community needs to decide where it wants to go and then how to get there."³¹

There are no models for Crested Butte to follow. As Thom Cox puts it plainly, "Every politician says, 'Well, I'm for growth, but I'm for controlled growth.' What does that really mean?" History shows that no matter how careful people think they are about growth, outside pressure usually wins out. John Hess points out that "Aspen was very sophisticated, but that didn't help much."

Many people's worst fear is that eventually Crested Butte will become another Aspen, where there has been chaotic growth and where most of the local residents have been gradually pushed out of town because they can no longer afford to live there. The result is a loss in community life, and the urban refugees who were trying to escape end up in a place little different from where they came from.

There are similar fears that Crested Butte will become like Telluride, which is even more isolated than Crested Butte, but has "been discovered" and today attracts a wealthier, more visible crowd. Remarkably, in 1991, the huge, multi-storied Doral Hotel development in Telluride was the second largest construction project in the state, topped only by the new international airport in Denver.³²

Bill Crank recognizes that people like him will probably have to leave Crested Butte if there is a boom: "If we get a big rush of interest from wealthier clientele, the likelihood of us getting forced out is pretty good." He says that, realistically, the people who have made Crested Butte their home can only control so much; they can deal with their own municipal problems, but the real threat is the intense pressure from the outside. Looking toward the future, Crank plainly states: "I am not optimistic at this point."³³

The ultimate question is whether Crested Butte can chart its own course and defy that of other ski towns. Sandy Fails does not see any point in thinking that the fate of Crested Butte is locked up. She says that people who believe that everything will change for the worse, no matter what they do, often "feel no hope and so they just give it up and enjoy the ride"; or, their constant worry impedes them from looking thoughtfully toward the future: "There's a difference between wanting to solve problems and being tied up in knots about where Crested Butte is going. Fretting is not the way to effect good, positive change."34

Gary Sprung says Crested Butte has an advantage in that it can benefit from observing other negative examples: "Crested Butte and the county are behind the rest of the resorts in Colorado, so we have the opportunity to learn." He is hopeful for the future because of all the resources Crested Butte has to draw from: "The public lands will remain public lands. We've managed to get a lot of wilderness area around Crested Butte. And there is a strong community. Although it is threatened by rich people, the community is still intact." For these reasons, says Gary, "We can move into the next century with a plan for a sustainable way of life here."35

The town is experimenting with different ways to preserve its community and way of life. The Crested Butte Land Trust is seeking opportunities to save open space, and the government has established other regulations and tax requirements that encourage land preservation and the building of affordable housing. George Sibley and others have started a local Chautauqua which brings people of different backgrounds and interests together to discuss the challenges facing the town and the surrounding area. The Chautauqua, George says, has as its guiding themes "sustainability and some

The new generation—Crested Butte Nursery School's annual bike tour, 1984

sense of social equity" and works to "address issues that are acknowledged and recognized by the community and make people think differently and more expansively. The goal is to change the way we approach problem solving in a community."[36]

When speculating about the town's future, people return again and again to the uniqueness of the place and the people who live here. Crested Butte has always been different, many say, and will therefore face the future differently. Sandy Fails draws hope from the fact that people in Crested Butte have never followed the well-travelled path: "People who live here have a special creative spark. They don't just accept the mainstream way of doing things. The notion that 'it's always been done this way' just doesn't carry as much weight here." Jim Schmidt adds that people in Crested Butte have always

The public lands will remain public lands. Oh-Be-Joyful Valley, northwest of town, was added to the Raggeds Wilderness area in 1993.

been more protective about their way of life and therefore have always demanded more from change: "Elsewhere, the mantra has always been 'Growth is good, growth is great.' Here, though, ever since I came to this valley, people have felt that growth should pay its own way."[37]

Maintaining the unique quality of Crested Butte will depend on the ability of the town to come up with creative ways to preserve as much open space as possible and to provide means for hard-working and contributing members of the community to be able to continue to live there. Gary Sporcich believes the strength of the people here and their commitment to the place will determine the future more than anything else: "The so-called Aspenization is more of an internal process than external. When the community loses focus on where we want to be, then you see other forces come in and take charge." He adds: "Internally, you either control that or let it happen to you. Not that you can control all of the forces that are at work here. But if you stand up to them, you'll have the ability to shape the change."³⁸

Sandy feels it is essential for people in Crested Butte to remember why they came here and why the sacrifices they have made to live here are so worthwhile. She says people who stay in touch with what attracted them to Crested Butte will be more committed to preserving what is

Sandy Fails and her son, Christopher, camping by Yule Lakes, north of Crested Butte.

here rather than wanting or allowing Crested Butte to become more like other places. Sandy gives a personal example: "I love it when people drive by in their fancy cars, look at me on my mountain bike, and *they* envy *me*. I imagine I'm a lot happier than a lot of them." What is so important, she continues, is for people "to keep remembering what's special about this town so that others, when they come here, will want to be a part of it. If we start doing battle with what we're not, we lose everything we value now."³⁹

There is reason to be hopeful when so many people who live here say that despite the increasing pressures for growth and development, they would not live anywhere else. They still consider themselves, in Glo Cunningham's words, to be among "the most blessed people on earth." Many residents also feel strongly that Crested Butte is a place that is not only loved and cared for

Crested Butte looking northwest up the Slate River valley toward Paradise divide, 1980

by those who live here, but that has the power to change others who come. As Jim Schmidt says, "The town just changes people's attitudes, it changes people's values, after they've been here for a while." Only such a special place as this has the promise of succeeding where other towns have gone wrong.[40]

Many ways of life have emerged in America, only to disappear and be forgotten. History is more recent in the West and is still in the making. The West continues to be a land of opportunity where people come to start their lives anew or attempt to make their fortunes.

In the mountains and valleys that give rise to the head waters of the Gunnison River and surround the town of Crested Butte, familiar forces that shaped Western history from the beginning are again in play. This time the exploitation takes the form of accelerated development reflecting recreation and population pressures. Economic interests largely from the outside tend, as ever, to be mindless of social dislocation and environmental costs.

Crested Butte so far maintains its own character and specialness. The question is whether it can continue to do so. As its residents debate their future, they might take encouragement from the town's own story, realizing that they are now playing a part in history in a continuum with the old-timers. The decisions they make and implement will mark the town as deeply as anything their predecessors did.

If the community can continue to draw on its traditional energy and spirit, it will be able to shape much of the change that is upon it and avert the most grievous damage. The efforts made toward these ends and the successes and failures that follow will not just affect the richness of life that presently nurtures the townspeople and their children; they will provide examples and precedents for other still undiscovered communities around the West.

The next chapter in this history of a Western town is in the making and as the end of the twentieth century approaches, heightening the significance of human concerns and transactions, it promises to be as defining as any in the past.

NAMES AND LIVES

Joe and Gwen Danni

Joe's grandfather came to the United States from Italy in 1895 and worked in New Mexico before moving to Crested Butte where he did mostly timber work. After he had made enough money to pay their passage, he sent for his wife and two children who were still in Italy, including Joe's father, Tony, who was only six or seven years old. They arrived in Crested Butte on March 27, 1897. Joe's father, Tony, grew up in Crested Butte and later opened a livery business that ran regular trips through Gothic, Schofield Park, and Crystal Canyon to Marble and as far as Redstone. When he returned from World War I in 1919, he moved down valley to ranch. Tony Danni was also elected to the Board of County Commissioners in 1944, on which he served for eighteen years.

Joe lived for most of his life in the house that his father built in 1936 along the East River several miles south of Crested Butte. He went to the local one-room schoolhouse with all of the other ranchers' children through the eighth grade and then attended high school in Gunnison. Joe spent all of his working life ranching. His wife, Gwen, grew up in Gunnison, but many of her relatives on her mother's side were from Crested Butte, and many of the men worked in the mines. Her father worked on the railroad. Gwen and Joe have two sons, Joe and Jerry. In 1992, Gwen and Joe sold their ranch property and the house that Joe's father built and moved to Gunnison.[1]

Johnny Krizmanich

Johnny Krizmanich lived in Crested Butte for seventy four years of his life, with four years in the army during World War II. His parents came to Crested Butte from Croatia, his father in 1895 or 1897, and his mother in 1902. Johnny's slight accent hints of the European influence in his upbringing. The death of his father when he was only eight years old left his mother with seven children to care for. His older brothers Tony and Stevie went to work in the mines when they were only fourteen or fifteen to help provide for the family. Johnny quit school in the eighth grade, started working in the CF&I Big Mine when he was eighteen, and worked there for seventeen years. After the mine closed in 1952, he was forced to leave his family for extended periods in order to find work elsewhere; for eighteen years, he continued to work in various mines, among them the Keystone Mine and Mill in Crested Butte, Thompson Creek, and Somerset. He and his wife June moved from Crested Butte to Gunnison in 1991.[2]

June Krizmanich

June Krizmanich is a third-generation Crested Butte resident. Her grandparents on both sides came to this country from Italy, and her mother, Lucy Marasco, was born and raised in Crested Butte in a family of fourteen children. June's father started picking slate at the Peanut Mine when he was only twelve and spent the rest of his working life in the mines. June came from an unusually small family compared to most old-timers; she had only two brothers, one of whom died in infancy during a flu epidemic. A few years after she and Johnny had their son, John, June went to work at Stefanic's Grocery, where she worked on and off for seventeen years. There she developed a reputation for giving very generous scoops of home-made ice cream to the local children.[3]

Matt Malensek

Born in 1901, Matt Malensek spent most of his life in Crested Butte until he moved down valley to a ranch with his wife, brother, and sister-in-law in 1971. He grew up in a family of four brothers and six sisters, three of whom died when they were very young. Matt was third-generation Slovenian, his grandfather and father having homesteaded Crested Butte Mountain together in 1901. His grandfather eventually returned to Slovenia, but Matt's father stayed and married another Slovene immigrant.

Matt's family operated the ranch up on Crested Butte mountain at an altitude of 9,000 to 10,000 feet for years before selling it in 1958 to developers of the ski area. Matt mined for twenty years and was very involved in unions from the start. He married Anne Mihelich, and eleven years later his brother Rudy married Anne's sister Margaret. Anne passed away in 1987, and Matt spent the last several years of his life living with Rudy and Margaret on another ranch outside Gunnison that is now run by Margaret and Rudy's son John. Matt passed away in the summer of 1991.[4]

Margaret and Rudy Malensek

Margaret Mihelich Malensek's parents came from Croatia; her father arrived first in 1883 and sent back for her mother. There were nine children in the family; two brothers and a sister died in childhood. Her third brother, Tony Mihelich, runs the famous Conoco Station on Elk Avenue, which he has been operating for over fifty years. Margaret worked for CF&I's Colorado Supply Store for twelve years before marrying Rudy. Rudy has spent most of his life ranching and they have two sons: John, who runs the ranch down the valley outside of Gunnison where Margaret and Rudy now live, and Anthony, who is a physicist in Illinois.[5]

Lyle McNeill

Born in Crested Butte in 1912, Lyle McNeill spent all but the last two years of his life in Crested Butte; he refused to leave even when his family moved away in 1935. Both of his parents were born in the United States, his mother in Illinois and his father in Colorado. They came to Crested Butte from Lafayette, Colorado, in 1911, and his father began working in the Big Mine soon thereafter. Lyle grew up in a family of five children. He seemed to have touched every aspect of Crested Butte: he peddled milk on a sleigh as a boy, mined in the Big Mine, operated his own heavy equipment contracting business, and served as mayor for nearly twenty six years—six before the Big Mine closed, and twenty thereafter. Lyle also served on the boards of local businesses, hospitals, and schools. He and his wife, Mildred, who is also a Crested Butte native, married in 1934 and have three children: Connie, Janice, and Sharon. Mildred and Lyle moved to Gunnison in the spring of 1991. Lyle passed away in the winter of 1993.[6]

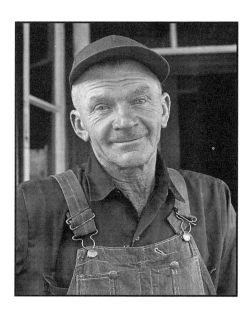

Tony Mihelich

Tony Mihelich, Margaret's brother, owns and operates the Crested Butte Hardware and Auto Supply and Conoco Station located on Elk Avenue. Perhaps the best-known building in Crested Butte, the Crested Butte Hardware and Auto Supply building was built in 1883 by John McCosker; in 1922 Tony's father-in-law, William H. Whalen, bought the store and Whalen's sons-in-law, Roger Nelson and John Camel, later took ownership. In 1939, a few years after Nelson was killed in a car accident going over Monarch Pass, Tony Mihelich married his widow, Helen Nelson, and started working in the hardware store. Tony never did work in the mines. His first real job after he quit the eighth grade was working as a delivery boy for M. R. Fisher. He then worked for a freight business and after that for the town before he went to work for the CB Hardware and Auto Supply. Tony's parents both came from Croatia, and he was born in Crested Butte in 1903. Out of the seven children in his family, four died when they were young. His sisters, Margaret and Ann, who married the Malensek brothers, Rudy and Matt, are his only two siblings who survived into old age. Going into the Conoco Station is in many ways like stepping back into time. Parts of the interior have never been changed, including Tony's coal stove, which is ninety years old and still heats the building all winter long. Tony is something of a legend; he has been featured in the Colorado news several times and is known by people all over the country who send him postcards and, when in town, stop by to chat. There is no possible way for Tony to remember the thousands of people he has met; as he says: "I meet so many people, day in and day out, it's hard to remember them all." But one thing is evident: they all remember him.[7]

Joe Saya

Joe Saya lived in Crested Butte on and off for eighty seven years. His father came to Crested Butte before the turn of the century and sent back to Croatia for Joe's mother after he had arrived and made some money. When they were young, Joe and his four brothers and three sisters lost their father to gangrene, which he got from an infection he contracted while working in the mines. In order to support her family, Joe's mother had to take in laundry, which she, like all the other women in town, washed daily on a scrubbing board. At seventeen, Joe lied about his age to get a job working in the coal mines. He worked in nearly all of the different mines that were operating in Crested Butte and eventually purchased the Peanut Mine, which he worked with one of his brothers for several years. After the Peanut shut down in 1955, he had to go elsewhere for work, but he always came back to Crested Butte. He had two sons, a daughter, and seven grandchildren. Joe passed away in 1992. The family still owns his house on Maroon Avenue and frequently returns to visit.[8]

Joe Sedmak

Joe still lives in the house where he was born and grew up with his three sisters and two brothers, one of whom died in infancy. Their parents came from Slovenia and, like so many other children of immigrants, they grew up speaking Slovenian at home. Joe started picking coal in the summertime at the age of ten. He worked for years in the mines, starting alongside his father at the age of eighteen in the Big Mine in 1932. After 1952, he stayed in Crested Butte, where he found various jobs with the county.[9]

Rudy Sedmak

Rudy Sedmak, Joe's older brother by three years, was born in 1912. He remembers that his grandfather, who came over from Slovenia around 1887, used to tell a story about when in 1887 or 1888 Crested Butte miners killed three Indians on top of the bench. Although Rudy started mining at the Horace Anthracite Mine—later called the Peanut—when he was sixteen, he was one of the few boys of his group of peers who went all the way through high school. Rudy married Emmy Verzuh, another Crested Butte native, and they had one child, Mary Jo, who still lives in Crested Butte and works as the librarian at the town library located in the Old Rock Schoolhouse. Rudy worked in the mines for thirty years, twenty six of them for CF&I. Around the time of World War II, when production was boosted and the work week was extended to six days, he worked nine years straight without missing a shift. After the Big Mine shut down, Rudy held a variety of jobs, including doing construction work on Indian reservations in New Mexico and Arizona, mining in the Thompson Creek Mine in Carbondale, cutting lumber for the Keystone Mine, and working as a caretaker for an estate in Aspen. After the ski area opened, Rudy was also the first operator of the T-Bar, which he ran for fifteen years before moving over to the Keystone chair, otherwise known as "Rudy's Lift."[10]

John and Frances Somrak

John Somrak, whose parents came from Slovenia, was born in 1914 and lived in Crested Butte for sixty nine years before moving to Gunnison with his wife, Frances, to work for the U.S. Forest Service. Like so many other Crested Butte old-timers, he lost his father in a mining accident when he was only nine. After his stepfather also died, John, who was twenty two at the time, took on the responsibility of raising his two half brothers, Joe and Frank. He worked in the Big Mine until it closed and then found various jobs, including mining at the Keystone Mine and Mill, doing construction and ranch work , and working for the U.S. Forest Service. John retired from the Forest Service in 1978 after twenty two years of service. He met his wife, Frances, at a dance when she was at Western State College in Gunnison getting her teaching certificate.[11]

Betty Spehar

Both of Betty Spehar's parents came from Croatia—her father arrived when he was two, her mother at age seventeen. Her father managed stores in different mining towns in the state before returning to Crested Butte, where he first managed a store for his cousin, Martin Verzuh, and then opened his own store, known as Spehar's. Betty and her five siblings used to spend weekends with their grandparents, who also lived in town and who insisted that the children perfect their Croatian language skills. Betty went on to college and graduate school and was away from Crested Butte from 1941 to 1952. She taught at the University of Colorado in Boulder from 1946 to 1950, traveled in Europe, and then came back when the Big Mine closed and taught in the local high school. She became a professor of English at Western State College in Gunnison in 1956. She now lives in the same Crested Butte house in which she grew up, which was originally the Pioneer Apartment Hotel. Her family still has some land in Croatia, where she visited in 1962, 1968, and 1989.[12]

Josephine Stajduhar

Josephine's parents came from Croatia in the late 1800s. Born and raised in Crested Butte, she grew up in a family of six sisters and one brother, who was killed in the Big Mine at the age of twenty three. Josephine quit school in ninth grade and, like many other girls, went to work cleaning houses. Many years later, after her three sons had left home, she worked at the first ski lodge up on Crested Butte Mountain. After the Big Mine closed, she and her husband and children had to move around the state so that her husband could find other mining jobs. They continued to return to Crested Butte, however, where Josephine still lives. In recent years, Josephine spent much of her time inside taking care of her husband, Renaldo, or Reny, who died of black lung on February 25, 1993. Josephine's sister Dorothy lives in Crested Butte, her sister Mary in Gunnison; their three other sisters visit them in the summertime.[13]

Tony and Eleanor Stefanic

Tony Stefanic is best known for the store that he and his wife, Eleanor, operated on Elk Avenue for about forty years. In the 1970s and early 1980s, Stefanic's and the Take Away, a branch of the Gunnison store owned by the Sweitzer family, were the only two grocery stores in town. Tony was born in 1913 in "Little Chicago," a camp located near Kebler Pass, between Irwin and Crested Butte. His parents came from Croatia in the early 1900s. His father worked in the Peanut, Floresta, and Buckley coal mines, until he was killed in a mining accident when Tony was twelve years old. Tony started working in grocery stores after he quit school at fourteen and owned his first store when he was twenty four. He met Eleanor Hardebeck, a Cincinnati native, on the train from Cincinnati to Greensburg, Indiana, while he was on his way home on leave from the navy during World War II. Tony sat down across from Eleanor and asked her, "How would you feel about writing to a lonely sailor?" She said she would. When Tony returned from the war in 1945, he and Eleanor got married in Indiana and moved to Crested Butte. Here they opened the store they would continuously operate for forty years until the end of December, 1985. Tony and Eleanor have three children: Marcia, Rose, and Anton Martin, better known as "Marty." Tony passed away January 31, 1994, and Eleanor moved to Gunnison the following summer. Stefanic's store still exists but is operated under different management.[14]

Martin "Teeny" Tezak

Teeny Tezak was born just outside of Crested Butte in the small mining community of Floresta, which became a ghost town a few years after he left in 1912 when he was only a year and a half old. He spent the rest of his life in Crested Butte until 1989, when he moved to Gunnison for health reasons. His parents came from Slovenia, a part of the Austro-Hungarian Empire, his father in 1904 and his mother in 1917. His mother's brothers had arrived first and arranged for her to marry someone else in town, but as Teeny says, "She liked Dad better, and they got married." His father died of cancer of the throat before Teeny's 13th birthday, leaving a family of nine children—three boys and six girls—and forcing his mother to take in boarders and laundry work. Teeny quit school after the eighth grade to work on ranches, including the Malensek Ranch up on Crested Butte Mountain. He also worked for a freight company, hauling groceries and mail to Gothic and Smith Hill. Teeny started work in the Big Mine when he was seventeen and in 1952, just before the mine shut down, went to work on the railroad and then took various jobs in the Crested Butte area.[15]

Fred Yaklich

Fred Yaklich, born in 1913, is a third-generation Crested Butte native. His mother's father, Jacob Kochevar, came from Slovenia in about 1876 and was one of the first settlers in Crested Butte from the republics of the Austro-Hungarian Empire. After arriving he sent for his wife, Marija Kochevar, who came across the ocean with her four children. Jacob Kochevar was a prospector who would leave home in the spring and not reappear until the fall. He discovered several deposits, including the Peanut and the Buckley, but never staked a claim for them. In addition to prospecting, he ran a general store on the same property where Fred and his wife Leola now live, which provided Crested Butte with supplies and also served as a post office. Jacob's wife, Marija, was a midwife for the Slovenian community and ran a boarding house for bachelor immigrants. They had two more children after they came to Crested Butte, including Fred's mother, Frances, who was born in 1890. Fred's father, Philip Yaklich, came to the U.S. when he was about seventeen years old and, after arriving in Crested Butte, he homesteaded the Meridian Lake property,

Daughters Trudy, Cindy, and Leola Yaklich

ran a bakery in town for several years, and started his own dairy. The middle son in a family of three boys and one girl, Fred started milking cows when he was six years old. He started working in the Peanut Mine when he was sixteen and then joined his father at the Buckley Mine when he was seventeen or eighteen. Fred finished high school in Crested Butte and spent two years studying at the University of Colorado in Boulder. He and his wife, Leola, who was living in Gunnison at the time, met at a dance in Almont; according to Leola, this was not uncommon: "The boys in Crested Butte came to Almont and of course the Gunnison girls came to meet them, because all the Crested Butte boys were good dancers." They were married in 1942. After serving a year in the navy during World War II, Fred came back to Crested Butte, quit his job in the Big Mine, and took over his father's dairy. At that time it was the only dairy in Crested Butte and reputed to be one of the best in the state, "highest in butterfat, lowest in bacteria count." It also served all the Civilian Conservation Corps camps in the area, shipping milk to Wyoming, Kansas, and Utah. Fred continued operating the dairy until 1960, and then went into construction work and plumbing with his friend and partner, Willard Ruggera. For a long time, they were the only plumbers in Crested Butte. Fred and Leola have four children, one son and three daughters.[16]

DATES AND FACTS

Bert Gross lived in Crested Butte in the early 1900s. One winter, on snowshoes, he delivered the mail nine miles to the town of Gothic.

Before the Europeans came, the Northern Utes, or Uncompahgre, were the original inhabitants of the Elk Mountain region and Gunnison River Valley. It is thought that ancient Ute culture originated from the northern migration of the Anasazis after they deserted Mesa Verde and other villages in the Four Corners area toward the end of the thirteenth century. Once controlling a vast domain that included large parts of Colorado, New Mexico, Utah, and Wyoming, the Utes are the only Native American tribe truly indigenous to the state of Colorado. Before being forced onto reservations, the Utes lived in the most rugged and remote areas of the Rocky Mountains and were known for their hardiness and independence.

The Arrival of the White Man

1820s and 1830s	Beaver trappers were the first white men to venture into the Rocky Mountains. They had limited contact with the Northern Utes of the Gunnison River Valley.
1848	War against Mexico ended Spanish dominance in North America.
	As part of the growing interest in western expansion into territory just opened up by the end of the war, Captain John Gunnison surveyed the Elk Mountain region of the Western Slope of Colorado for a railroad route between the 38th and 39th parallels. He was unable to find a viable route, and in the winter of 1848–1849 was killed in Utah by a band of Piutes. The town of Gunnison, twenty eight miles south of Crested Butte, was named for him.

Panning for gold

Gold and Silver Mining

1859 After the discovery of gold in Cherry Creek in 1858, Auraria and Denver were established as sister towns to accommodate the growing number of prospectors. The rush to Colorado resulted in mounting pressure on Ute territories.

1861 White men began gold mining in Minersville, a settlement in Ute territory just a few miles north of the future townsite of Crested Butte. In 1861, the population of Minersville was 200 and by 1862 there were one thousand prospectors in the Washington Gulch area. That summer most fled after twelve miners were killed by Utes.

Territory of Colorado was established on the eve of the Civil War.

1868 Treaty with the Utes left them the western third of Colorado.

1873   Brunot Treaty with the Utes took away one fourth of the remaining Ute land in Colorado, or an additional four million acres. Miners rushed into the Gunnison area. Hayden named Crested Butte while surveying the area.

1876   On August 1, President U. S. Grant declared Colorado an official state.

1860s and 1870s   In the frenzied search for gold and silver, mining towns appeared overnight in Elk Mountain region with names like Gothic, Ruby-Irwin, Oh-Be-Joyful, Washington and Poverty Gulches, Peeler, Pittsburg, and Elkton; in the winter of 1879–1880, the Gunnison area was talked about all over the U.S. By 1880, Gunnison was a boom town.

Coal Mining

1878   Anticipating the importance of local coal deposits, a man named Howard Smith officially laid out the town of Crested Butte. He had purchased the coal land around Coal Creek, which ran through the camp the year before. He went on to build a sawmill and smelter in 1879. Crested Butte served as the supply center for the various hard-rock mining camps in the Elk Mountain region; hundreds of burros often stood on Elk or Maroon Avenues waiting to be loaded with goods to be transported to the more remote settlements.

1880   Crested Butte was formally incorporated on July 3. The town's population was four hundred, and one thousand additional miners lived within a three-mile radius. A few coal mines had been developed, and local coke ovens turned coal into coke, a valuable source of fuel produced by the burning of bituminous coal in order to drive out its volatile parts.

A final treaty forced all Northern Utes onto reservations in Utah; Southern Utes were allowed to remain on a small reservation in southwestern Colorado.

1881 The Denver and Rio Grande (D&RG) railroad won its race to Gunnison against the Denver South Park Railroad, and at noon on November 21, the first D&RG train rolled into Crested Butte. The arrival of the railroads ended the extreme isolation of the Western Slope region, and the D&RG soon owned much of the coal land in Crested Butte. The railroad supplied the inexpensive, year-round transportation so essential to the development of coal mining in Crested Butte.

1882 The population of Crested Butte reached one thousand, with five hotels, a bank, and a dozen saloons.

1883 The Colorado Coal & Iron Company (CC&I) owned and leased over two thousand acres of land in and around Crested Butte. CC&I went on to build over 150 beehive ovens for the production of coke. Coal from the mines was loaded into the ovens, and the coke was removed a few days later and put into railroad cars which carried the coke as far as Denver, Pueblo, and Salt Lake City.

Looking north on Main Street from Tomichi Avenue in Gunnison, a boom town by 1880

Preparing the railroad bed for construction of the track

1890s   New immigration occurred. Before 1895, most of the residents of Crested Butte were Anglo-Saxon. In the 1890s, southeastern European Catholic Slavic, Croatian, and Italian immigrants started to arrive, transforming the population of the town.

1891   CC&I opened the Jokerville Mine, which employed 100 to 120 miners day and night.

The first strike in Crested Butte caused a skirmish with the Gunnison County Sheriff, but there were no injuries.

Crested Butte had 154 coke ovens. Coke was made by heating coal until it was red hot for several days. Then it was taken by train to the CF&I plant in Pueblo to make steel. Coke burned more intensely than coal and produced less smoke.

1892 CC&I merged with the Colorado Fuel Company to form Colorado Fuel and Iron (CF&I), the mining corporation which would dominate coal mining and many other aspects of life in Crested Butte for nearly sixty years.

1893 The demonetization of silver brought the panic of 1893. All of the hard-rock mining camps around Crested Butte, which had always been prone to dramatic fluctuation, markedly declined. By 1900, Gothic's population, which was recorded as 949 in 1880, had dwindled to fifty; and Irwin's population, which was 1,123 in 1880, had dropped to ninety two. Meanwhile, the less appealing, less romantic mining of coal allowed Crested Butte to survive in the midst of ghost towns.

1894 The Jokerville mine exploded, killing sixty miners. It was Colorado's worst mining disaster to date.

CF&I opened the Big Mine, which by 1902 employed four hundred people and was producing one thousand tons of coal per day. Crested Butte would grow to depend on the Big Mine for its major source of income for the next fifty years.

High temperatures and toxic fumes made the production of coke dangerous work. In 1918, the use of coke was replaced by natural gas and the coke ovens were closed.

1900 — Crested Butte and Gunnison were the only major towns left in the region; Crested Butte had a population of 988, and Gunnison a population of 1,200.

1912 — Coal production in Colorado reached its peak; after this time, it declined until World War II.

1913 to 1914 — The United Mine Workers of America (UMW of A) organized the coal miners of Colorado. In April 1914 at Ludlow, another mining town in the state, nineteen people were killed by National Guardsmen; the infamous event became known as the "Ludlow Massacre." In Crested Butte, 275 miners had joined the state-wide strike. There was no violence, but the strike lasted eighteen months and gained little for the miners.

1918 — Coke production in Crested Butte ended.

Increased demand for fuel during World War I raised coal production, but not by significant amounts. In the 1920s, the market for coal experienced a slight depression because of excess supply and increased competition from other forms of energy.

1927 The last major strike occurred in Crested Butte because of a twenty percent cut in wages. The miners were assisted by the International Workers of the World (IWW). They returned to work after several months with none of their demands satisfied.

1931 Crested Butte Bank failed. Until then, the Depression had not hit hard in town.

1940 to 1945 Coal production had climbed to over 200 thousand tons in 1940. With an increased national demand for coal, the Big Mine went to a a six-day week. The high level of production was maintained until 1945. CF&I experienced a shortage of labor and was forced to close some of its smaller mines in order to keep the Big Mine operating.

1952 The Big Mine closed after nearly sixty years of operation.

The American Smelting and Refining Company built Keystone Mine and Mill on the side of Mt. Emmons. The mine produced lead, zinc, copper, and silver and provided many needed jobs until it closed in 1969.

1954 The Denver & Rio Grande railroad closed its line to Crested Butte, and picked up its tracks.

The Rise of Recreation

1962   Two years after purchasing the Malensek Ranch on Crested Butte Mountain, two Kansans, Dick Eflin and Fred Rice, opened the Crested Butte ski area.

1965   The ski area went bankrupt this year and the following year.

1970   The ski area was sold to the Crested Butte Development Corporation headed by Howard "Bo" Callaway, a wealthy Georgia businessman.

1972   Newcomers swept local elections in town, forcing out Lyle McNeill and other old-timers.

1973   The separate town of Mt. Crested Butte was incorporated, located just below the ski area three miles north of town.

1974   Crested Butte was designated a National Historic District.

1977 AMAX, an international mining conglomerate, announced plans to mine molybdenum ore at Mt. Emmons three miles west of Crested Butte. The proposal encountered fierce opposition from many of the townspeople who had recently moved to town and wanted to protect their new lifestyle in the mountains. The opponents of AMAX, led by the town mayor, also a newcomer, eventually won a long and hard-fought battle.

1980s Crested Butte suffered from the oil recession. However, in the late 1980s, tourism started to grow rapidly, and the real estate market picked up again. The town and surrounding area experienced a boom in recreation expansion.

1990s Crested Butte gains popularity as a ski area and is held to be the mountain bike capital of the world. There is talk about the opening of more slopes on Snodgrass Mountain next to Crested Butte Mountain. Development in town continues, and the community works hard to prevent the kind of uncontrolled growth that has occurred in other ski towns in Colorado and around the country.

ENDNOTES

Preface

1 population records from Crested Butte Town Hall.

Beginnings

1 rich reward—Robert G. Athearn, *The Coloradans* (Albuquerque: University of New Mexico Press, 1976), 65–68.; in 1873—Duane Vandenbusche, *The Gunnison Country* (Gunnison, CO: B&B Printers, Gunnison, Inc., 1980), 20.

2 surrounding camps—Vandenbusche, 203; boom town—Ibid, 125–127.

3 demonetization of silver—Ibid, 431.

4 Ibid, 202.

The Emigrants

1 Danni, interview by author, 2 July 1991.

2 turn of the century—Smith, *When Coal Was King* (Golden: Colorado School of Mines Press, 1984), 63.

3 Croatia and Slovenia—Michele Veltri, *We Are All Brothers: The Slavic Fraternal Lodges of Crested Butte* (Paonia, CO: Hubbard Printing, 1980), 9; make up Yugoslavia—George Prpic, *South Slavic Immigration in America* (Boston: Twayne Publishers, a Division of G.K. Hall & Co.), 66–67.

4 United States—Prpic, *Slavic Immigration*, 41–42; 53–54.; 1880 to 1914—Susel, Rudolph, "Slovenes," *Harvard Encyclopedia of American Ethnic Groups*, 934–935.

5 Western United States—Prpic, 85; was Crested Butte—Ibid, 136; and Leadville—Veltri, *Fraternal Lodges*, 10.

6 Smith, *When Coal Was King*, 63–64.

7 Johnny Krizmanich, interview by author, 28 November 1990.

8 John Somrak, interview by author, 27 March 1991.

9 "No—this is my home"—Johnny Krizmanich, interviews by author; "She never did go back"—Martin Tezak, interview by author 25 March 1991, 1 July 1991.

The Immigrants

1 "different types"—Joe Saya, interview by author, 1 July 1991; "end of the street"—Rudy Sedmak, interview by author, 21 August 1995; on the town—Smith, *When Coal Was King*, 63.

2 "spit in the bucket"—Saya, interview by author; "Jajcers" and "Cousin Jacks"—Betty Spehar, interview by author, 9 July 1991; "a Cousin Jack"—Rudy Sedmak, interview by author.

3 "stuff to eat"—John Somrak, interview by author.

4 Fred and Leola Yaklich, interview by author, 8 July 1993.

5 Betty Spehar, interview by author.

6 Veltri, *Fraternal Lodges*, 12–14.

7 "insurance purposes"—Rudy Sedmak, interview by author; "badges and everything"—Saya, interview by author; "an insurance company"—Yaklich, interview by author.

8 "really lovely"—Spehar, interview by author; information on lodges from Veltri, *Fraternal Lodges*, 22.

9 Catholic Church information from Vandenbusche, *The Gunnison Country*, 229.

10 "work together"—John Somrak, interview by author; "had to be Protestant"—Johnny Krizmanich, interview by author.

11 "died down"—Fred Yaklich, interview by author.

12 "as anybody else"—Betty Spehar, interview by author.

13 "started from there"—John Somrak, interview by author.

14 "in the summer"—Tony Mihelich, interview by author, 10 July 1993; Krizmanich school information from Veltri, *Fraternal Lodges*, 17.

15 American history—Scamehorn, 55; work and ambition—Ibid, 155; information on coke from Smith, *When Coal Was King*, 8; "overtakes him"—*Camp & Plant*, publication of Colorado Fuel & Iron, 1928 issue.

16 "Austria-Hungary"—Johnny Krizmanich, interview by author, 25 March 1991.

17 "used to parade"—Saya, interview by author.

18 "that was okay"—Matt Malensek, interview by author, 17 July 1991.

19 "dropped out"—Johnny Krizmanich, interview by author, 25 March 1991; "Croatian Hall"—Rudy Sedmak, interview by author.

The Work

1 "Just to help"—Yaklich, interview by author.

2 "care of me"—Rudy Sedmak, interview by author.

3 "and then come back . . ."—Tezak, interview by author, 25 March 1991.

4 "railroad cars"—Yaklich, interview by author.

5 "main line"—Rudy Sedmak, interview by author.

6 "20, 22 inches"—Yaklich, interview by author.

7 "when it's dark"—Joe Sedmak, interview by author, 28 March 1991.

8 "long at it"—Yaklich, interview by author.

9 "brass identification"—Johnny Krizmanich, interview by author, 28 November 1990; "full of coal"—Rudy Sedmak, interview by author.

10 "nickel"—Yaklich, interview by author.

11 Vandenbusche, *The Gunnison Country*, 212.

12 "all the odds"—John Somrak, interview by author.

13 "up on the motors"—Tezak, interview by author, 25 March 1991.

14 Scamehorn, 5.

15 six thousand men—Ibid, 126; on the company—Smith, *When Coal Was King*, 51; educational and social services—Scamehorn, 126–127.

16 true company town—Smith, *When Coal Was King*, 51; privately owned—Ibid, 65.

17 "a week, nothing"—John Somrak, interview by author.

18 "mine entrance"—Yaklich, interview by author.

19 "survived on"—Mihelich, interview by author.

20 "their ways"—Johnny Krizmanich, interview by author, 28 November 1990.

21 Smith, *When Coal Was King*, 59.

22 "made the same"—Johnny Krizmanich, interview by author; "wanted to"—Yaklich, interview by author.

23 "English people"—Krizmanich, interview by author; "kept pushing them"—Yaklich, interview by author.

24 "something like that"—Yaklich, interview by author; "to the boss"—Johnny Krizmanich, interview by author, 25 March 1991; information on English supervisors and bosses from Smith, *When Coal Was King*, 60.

25 "a dollar or two"—Tezak, interview by author, 25 March 1991.

26 "buck it too"—John Somrak, interview by author.

27 people's lives—Scamehorn, 149.

28 "or awards"—Rudy Sedmak, interview by author.

29 Smith, *When Coal Was King*, 56.

30 "around the streets . . ."—Saya, interview by author.

31 "was forgotten"—Yaklich, interview by author.

32 Smith, 81.

33 information on Rockefeller Plan from Scamehorn, 129; "they would do"—John Somrak, interview by author.

34 "you nothing"—Saya, interview by author.

35 "at that time"—Margaret Malensek, interview by author, 2 July 1991.

36 "to the union"—Matt Malensek, interview by author, 17 July 1991.

37 "you'd quit"—Yaklich, interview by author.

38 "unions came in"—Johnny Krizmanich, interview by author, 25 March 1991.

39 "prejudice against"—Tezak, interview by author, 25 March 1991; "qualifications then"—Somrak, interview by author.

40 "later on"—Johnny Krizmanich, interview by author, 28 November 1990.

41 "just liked it"—Johnny Krizmanich, interview by author, 28 November 1990.

42 "dangerous work"—Saya, interview by author.

43 Smith, 108.

44 "in the mines"—Mihelich, interview by author.

45 "walked out"—Yaklich, interview by author.

46 "do better"—Tony and Eleanor Stefanic, interview by author.

47 "with the banks"—Tony and Eleanor Stefanic, interview by author.

48 "money, too"—Margaret Malensek interview, 17 July 1991; "the same"—Josephine Stajduhar, interview by author, 1 July 1991.

49 "health care, insurance"—Eleanor and Tony Stefanic, interview by author.

50 "work hard"—Eleanor and Tony Stefanic, interview by author.

The Life

1 "scrubbing board"—Mihelich, interview by author.

2 "it worked"—Yaklich, interview by author.

3 "helping somebody"—Joe and Gwen Danni, interview by author.

4 "terrible days"—Saya, interview by author.

5 "veils and all"—John Somrak, interview by author.

6 "come home"—Margaret Malensek, interview by author, 17 July 1991.

7 "you was home"—Josephine Stajduhar, interview by author, 1 July 1991.

8 "ten years old"—Sedmak, interview by author; "the boys"—Mihelich, interview by author.

9 "you survived on"—John Somrak, interview by author.

10 "at the stores"—Johnny Krizmanich, interview by author, 25 March 1991.

11 information on local bank from Smith, *When Coal Was King*, 107–108.

12 "to eat"—Yaklich, interview by author; "where they're at"—Tezak, interview by author, 1 July 1991.

13 "so ashamed"—Tezak, interview by author, 1 July 1991.

14 "dumplings"—Spehar, interview by author.

15 "can't swim!"—Stajduhar, interview by author, 1 July 1991.

16 "week to week"—Mihelich, interview by author.

17 "the money . . ."—June Krizmanich, interview by author.

18 "the sick person"—Spehar, interview by author.

19 "Crested Butte was"—John Somrak, interview by author.

20 "don't know why"—June Krizmanich, interview by author, 28 November 1990.

21 "your friends"—Johnny Krizmanich, interview by author, 28 November 1990.

22 "the other out"—Tezak, interview by author, 25 March 1991; "flung together"—Margaret Malensek, interview by author, 17 July 1991.

23 "on top"—Spehar, interview by author; "really nice"—Josephine Stajduhar, interview by author, 26 March 1991.

Snow: A Transition

1 "feet deep"—Saya, interview by author.

2 "the car again"—Sedmak, interview by author; "the horse out"—Yaklich, interview by author.

3 "buck the road"—Sedmak, interview by author.

4 "wonderful time"—Lyle McNeill, interview by author, 26 November 1990.

5 "skis'd break"—Saya, interview by author.

6 "ski very much"—Saya, interview by author; "a day"—Mihelich, interview by author.

Ski Town—Transformation

1 Scamehorn, 169.

2 energy sources—Smith, *When Coal Was King*, 119–122.

3 "going to close"—Eleanor Stefanic, interview by author; "to the town"—Tony Mihelich, interview by author; "Crested Butte"—Lyle McNeill, interview by author; "all scattered"—Margaret Malensek, interview by author, 1 July 1991.

4 "seventh heaven"—Stajduhar, interview by author, 26 March 1991.

5 "finished"—Tezak, interview by author, 25 March 1991; "tourists then"—Eleanor Stefanic, interview by author.

6 "make a living"—Mihelich, interview by author.

7 "they closed"—Tezak, interview by author, 25 March 1991.

8 "Crested Butte"—Saya, interview by author; "somethin' different"—John Somrak, interview by author.

9 "work as mining"—Johnny Krizmanich, interview by author, 28 November 1990.

10 "leave Crested Butte"—Rudy Sedmak, interview by author.

11 "grand time"—Spehar, interview by author.

12 "better conditions"—Mihelich, interview by author; "one you left"—Yaklich, interview by author.

13 Rudy Sedmak, interview by author.

14 George Sibley, author and historian, interview by author, telephone, 25 September 1991.

15 in operation—Vandenbusche, *Gunnison Country*, 227; after that—Dick Eflin, interview by author, telephone, 27 September 1991.

16 information on population fluctuations in town of Crested Butte from Crested Butte Town Hall; information on population fluctuations in town of Mt. Crested Butte from Mt. Crested Butte Town Hall.

17 Rudy Sedmak, interview by author.

18 "have something"—Spehar, interview by author; "like it"—Stajduhar, interview by author, 26 March 1991; "that way"—Johnny Krizmanich, interview by author, 28 November 1990.

19 "for business"—Mihelich, interview by author. "Crested Butte"—John Somrak, interview by author; "becomes dormant"—McNeill, interview by author.

The New People

1 "hippie element"—Johnny Krizmanich, interview by author, 28 November 1990; "Uh uh"—Stajduhar, interview by author, 26 March 1991.

2 "rough bunch"—June Krizmanich, interview by author.

3 "never do that"—June Krizmanich, interview by author; "from me"—Stajduhar, interview by author, 26 March 1991.

4 "noticed them"—Mihelich, interview by author; "were used to"—Yaklich, interview by author.

5 "friction is"—Danni, interview by author; "honest living"—Johnny Krizmanich, interview by author, 28 November 1990.

6 "had to go"—Malensek, interview by author, 1 July 1991.

7 "by with"—Malensek, interview by author, 1 July 1991.

8 "fun town"—Stajduhar, interview by author.

9 "whole life"—Yaklich, interview by author.

10 "make it"—Stajduhar, interview by author.

11 Stefanic, interview by author.

12 "a nickel now"—Malensek, interview by author, 1 July 1991.

13 "like I said"—Malensek, interview by author, 1 July 1991.

14 "relief even"—Tezak, interview by author, 1 July 1991.

15 "never work"—Sedmak, interview by author; "times of living"—Tezak, interview by author, 1 July 1991.

The Power Shift

1 "sit still"—*Crested Butte Chronicle*, 19 June 1968, 1.

2 "coming in"—Sedmak, interview by author; information on age of locals from "Basic Studies and Research Final Report 1973" of Crested Butte Planning Department, 1973.

3 "into the future"—Miles Rademan, city planner of Park City, Utah, interview by author, telephone, 3 October 1991.

4 "had passed by"—Rademan, interview by author.

5 "used to before"—Saya, interview by author.

6 information on Home Rule from David Leinsdorf.

7 "so what?"—John Somrak, interview by author; "wrecked Crested Butte"—Stajduhar, interview by author, 26 March 1991.

8 "set by Home Rule"—Yaklich, interview by author.

9 "us at all"—Yaklich, interview by author.

10 Home Rule information from Crank, interview by author, 4 October 1991.

11 "friends of mine"—Crank, interview by author.; "five years"—Rademan, interview by author.

12 "do something"—Rademan, interview by author.

13 "guys, you know"—John Somrak, interview by author.

14 "you are here"—Yaklich, interview by author.

15 information on citizen participation from Crested Butte Planning Department's "Basic Studies and Research Final Report" of 1973.

16 information on AMAX plans from article by David Sumner, "AMAX Comes to Crested Butte," *Sierra Magazine* (September/October 1979): 22–27.

17 "in Crested Butte"—Rademan, interview by author.

18 information on Mitchell and result of AMAX fight from W Mitchell, interview by author, telephone, 26 September 1991.

19 Mitchell, interview by author.

20 "natural environment?"—Joanne Ditmer, "Preservationists call Crested Butte 'Hottest issue,'" *Denver Post*, 10 December 1978, 37–38.

21 for $25,000—Tom Huth, "Crested Butte: A Town Fights for Its Heritage," *Historic Preservation* 31, no. 1 (Mar/Apr 1979): 4–8; "their lifestyle"—Smith and Vandenbusche, *Land Alone*, 242.

22 information on molybdenum mining and Leadville from Huth article, 4.
information on social implications from Ditmer article; "boom town?"—Mitchell, interview by author.

23 "here either"—John Somrak, interview by author.

24 "a community"—McNeill, interview by author; "and Leadville"—Tezak, interview by author, 1 July 1991.

25 "there now"—Johnny Krizmanich, interview by author, 28 November 1990; "than it is"—Spehar, interview by author.

26 "town today"—Sedmak, interview by author.

27 "same shape"—Tezak, interview by author, 1 July 1991; "to do it"—Fred Yaklich, interview by author.

28 "it from?"—Stefanic, interview by author.

29 "for that"—Yaklich, interview by author.

30 information on AMAX battle from Mitchell, interview by author.

31 "But they are"—Johnny Krizmanich, interview by author, 28 November 1991; "working class"—Danni, interview by author.

32 "built the town"—Saya, interview by author; "anything like that"—Spehar, interview by author.

33 "an affront"—Mitchell, interview by author; "whole lives"—Rademan, interview by author; "Gillette, Wyoming"—Mitchell, interview by author.

34 "that's it"—Danni, interview by author.

35 "never do that"—Johnny Krizmanich, interview by author, 28 November 1991; "element? No"—Spehar, interview by author.

36 "*no* before"—Mitchell, interview by author.

Recreation, Festivals, Tourists

1 "is all"—Tezak, interview by author, 1 July 1991; "for nothing"—Sedmak, interview by author; "on now" Stefanic, interview by author.

2 "doing good"—Saya, interview by author.

3 "know nobody"—Saya, interview by author; "how I feel"—Stajduhar, interview by author, 26 March 1991.

4 "that's all"—Johnny Krizmanich, interview by author, 28 November 1991.

5 "kinds of work"—Tezak, interview by author, 1 July 1991; "way it was"—John Somrak, interview by author.

6 "lose everything"—McNeill, interview by author; "for the town"—Mihelich, interview by author.

7 Danni, interview by author.

8 Dora Mae Trampe, interview by author, tape recording, Gunnison, Colorado, 1 July 1991.

9 "about it"—Trampe, interview by author.

10 "too small"—Danni, interview by author.

The Challenges

1 "gloriously beautiful"—Spehar, interview by author.

2 George Sibley, interview by author, 9 August 1995; Glo Cunningham, interview by author, 16 August 1995; Thom Cox, interview by author, 15 August 1995.

3 Jim Schmidt, interview by author, 16 August 1995; Sandy Fails, interview by author, 17 August 1995; Gary Sprung, interview by author, 15 August 1995.

4 Gary Sporcich, interview by author, 21 August 1995.

5 Glo Cunningham, interview by author, 16, August 1995.

6 Sandy Fails, interview by author.

7 Gary Sporcich, interview by author.

8 Sandy Fails, interview by author.

9 George Sibley, interview by author, 9 August 1995.

10 Glo Cunningham, interview by author.

11 Glo Cunningham, interview by author.

12 "real community here"—Jim Schmidt, interview by author; "the most from it"—Sandy Fails, interview by author.

13 Sandy Fails, interview by author.

14 George Sibley, interview by author.

15 George Sibley, interview by author.

16 "like that"—Jim Schmidt, interview by author; "any other place"—Gary Sporcich, interview by author.

17 Gary Sprung, interview by author.

18 "'not give to it'"—Jim Schmidt, interview by author; "big bucks"—Glo Cunningham, interview by author.

19 "sense of permanence"—Sandy Fails, interview by author; "soul of the town"—Jim Schmidt, interview by author.

20 Crank, interview by author, October 1991.

21 Gary Sporcich, interview by author.

22 "it is changing"—Sandy Fails, interview by author; "you can't buy"—George Sibley, interview by author, 9 August 1995.

23 "things you can"—George Sibley, interview by author, 9 August 1995; "change is implemented"—Gary Sporcich, interview by author.

24 "think we can"—Tom Cox, interview by author; George Sibley, interview by author, 9 August 1995.

25 "pay for it"—Jim Schmidt, interview by author.

26 "should compromise"—Gary Sprung, interview by author.

27 "my prediction"—Lyle McNeill, interview by author.

28 "going to happen"—Tony Mihelich, interview by author; "don't mean nothing"—Teeny Tezak, interview by author; "it is right now"—Johnny Krizmanich, interview by author.

29 "build all over"—Joe Saya, interview by author.

30 "Property around here"—Fred and Leola Yaklich, interview by author.

31 "things crazy"—Jim Schmidt, interview by author; "how to get there"—John Hess, City Planner, interview by author, telephone, 30 September 1991.

32 "really mean?"—Thom Cox, interview by author; "help much"—John Hess, interview by author.

33 Bill Crank, interview by author.

34 Sandy Fails, interview by author.

35 Gary Sprung, interview by author.

36 George Sibley, interview by author, 9 August 1995.

37 "weight here"—Sandy Fails, interview by author; "its own way"—Jim Schmidt, interview by author.

38 Gary Sporcich, interview by author.

39 Sandy Fails, interview by author.

40 "for a while"—Jim Schmidt, interview by author.

Names and Dates

1 Joe and Gwen Danni, interview by author.

2 Johnny Krizmanich, interviews by author, 28 November 1990, 25 March 1991.

3 June Krizmanich, interview by author, 25 March 1991.

4 Margaret, Matt, and Rudy Malensek, interview by author; Matt Malensek, interview by author.

5 Margaret, Matt, and Rudy Malensek, interview by author.

6 Lyle McNeill, interview by author.

7 Tony Mihelich, interview by author.

8 Joe Saya, interview by author.

9 Joe Sedmak, interview by author.

10 Rudy Sedmak, interview by author.

11 John Somrak, interview by author.

12 Betty Spehar, interview by author.

13 Josephine Stajduhar, interview by author.

14 Tony and Eleanor Stefanic, interview by author.

15 Martin "Teeny" Tezak, interview by author.

16 Fred and Leola Yaklich, interview by author.

CREDITS

Anderton, Susan illustrations: pp. viii, 7, 97, 101, 149, 177, 203.

Bailey, Michael maps: pp. i, 4, 10, 14.

Billow, Nathan photograph: p. 171.

Colorado Fuel and Iron photographs: pp. 7, 35, 42, 43 (*top* and *bottom*), 45, 47, 93.

Colorado Historical Society photographs: pp. 6, 34, 54, 59, 68, 80, 203.

Courtner, Sandra photographs: back endsheet, pp. 23, 98, 99, 100, 102, 111, 112, 113, 115, 116, 117, 120, 121 (*bottom*), 122, 123, 124, 125, 126, 127, 128, 129, 130, 132, 135, 142, 145, 146, 152, 153, 156, 157, 168, 174, 179, 180, 181, 182, 184, 185, 186, 188, 191, 193, 194, 195.

Crested Butte Pilot photograph: p. 89.

Danni, Gwen and Joseph photographs: p. 13.

Demerson, Dusty photograph: back cover, p. 39.

Denver Public Library photographs: front endsheet, pp. 5, 39, 44, 48, 51, 53, 76 (*bottom*), 87, 160, 202.

Frank Leslie's Illustrated Newspaper, January 5, 1884: p. 57.

Gunnison Camera Center photographs: pp. 12, 20, 27, 33, 60, 69.

Gunnison County Times photographs: pp. 90, 91, 104, 107, 121, 141, 207.

Harpers Weekly prints: pp. 40, 41.

Hegeman, Alan photograph: p. 103.

Johns, Dennis W. photograph: p. 173.

Nash, Honeydew photographs, courtesy of: p. 155, 171.

Pioneer Museum photographs: pp. 17, 18, 24, 26, 37, 75 (*bottom*), 205.

Reaman, Mark photographs: pp. 140, 144, 161, 165, 167.

Rozman, June and Ed photographs: pp. 22, 38, 72, 73, 86, 88.

Saya, Joe photographs: pp. 66, 74.

Somrak, Frances and John photograph, courtesy of: p. 189.

Vandenbusche, Duane photograph: p. 11

Western State College, Savage Library photographs: pp. 21, 30, 63, 78, 79, 197.

Wirth, Kelsey photographs: pp. 183, 187, 190, 192.

Wirth, Wren photographs: author (*back flap*), pp. ii, iii, 64, 74, 162, 165.

Yaklich, Carol and Phil photograph: p. 76 (*bottom*)

217

INDEX

A

accidents 40, 45, 67
Aerial Weekend 143, (*photo*) 145
after the fire, Ludlow (*photo*) 53
AMAX (formerly American Metal Climax, Inc.) 126–134, 137, 138, 208
American Smelting and Refining Company 103
Americanization 27, 28
Arts Fair (*photo*) 115, 143, 144
Aspen 169

B

banking 59
Baumgartner, Bruce 120, 130
being accepted (*photo*) 155
Big Mine, *See* CF&I, Big Mine
births 64
BKR Associates 120
Block, Ernestine (*photo*) 27
Block, Joseph H. (*photo*) 69
brass life check (*photo*) 39
bribery 48
Brower, David (*photo*) 132
Brunot Treaty 3, 201
Buckley Mine 44

C

Camp & Plant 27, 49
Callaway, Howard "Bo" 106, 207
Catholic 23–25, 31
CF&I, *See* Colorado Fuel & Iron Company
Chautauqua 171
Chocolate Peak 24
coal carts 34, 35, 36, 37, 38, (*photo*) 43
coal check 39
coal mine entry (*photo*) 44
coke ovens (*photo*) 204, 205
Colorado Coal & Iron Company (CC&I) 202
Colorado Fuel and Iron Company (CF&I) 5, 27, 41, 42, 43, 44, 46, 47, 49, 51, 55, 56, 204
    Big Mine 34, (*photo*) 34, 36, 40, 43, (*photo*) 45, 73, 204
    Big Mine closure 95–97, 206
    Colorado Supply Store (*photo*) 42, 47, (*photo*) 112
    company town 42, 43
    Home Safety chapter 49
Colorado Supply service station (*photo*) 48
communion class (*photo*) 75
construction 108

Cortner, Sandra 154
cousin Jacks 19
Cox, Thom (*photo*) 125
Crank, Bill 119, (*photo*) 125, 156
credit 76
Crested Butte (*photo*) 160, 174
Crested Butte Athletic Club 23
Crested Butte Bank 59
    explosion 157
Crested Butte Chronicle 158
Crested Butte House 17
Crested Butte Land Trust 171
Crested Butte Mountain Theatre (*photo*) 158
Crested Butte Nursery School (*photo*) 171
Croatia 10, 12
Croatian Hall 23
Croatian lodge 23
Cunningham, Glo 152
cutting timber (*photo*) 37

D

Danni family (*photo*) 13
Danni, Gwen 135, (*photo*) 179
Danni, Joe 9, 179, (*photo*) 179
Denver and Rio Grande Railway Company
    (D&RG) 5, 95, 202, 206
The Denver Post 129, 130
development 121

E

early snow-making (*photo*) 91
Eflin, Dick 105
egg eaters 19
Elk Avenue (*photos*): 11, 18, 21, 30, 38, 96, 117,
    124, 126, 162
Elk Cafe and Bar (*photo*) 73
Elk Mountain House 12
Elk Mountain Pilot 20
Elkton 3
environment 133, 134
epidemics 64
ethnic neighborhoods 16
european customs 31

F

Fails, Christopher (*photo*) 173
Fails, Sandy 152, (*photo*) 173

Fat Tire Bike Week (*photo*) 140, 143
Father McKenna (*photo*) 104
Fire Department Hose Team 29
Flaushink Festival (*photo*) 166
Floresta Mine 50
foot race (*photo*) 30
Forest Queen Mine (*photo*) 36
four generations (*photo*) 168
Fourth of July (*photo*) 27, (*photo*) 29, (*photo*) 30 ,
    143
Franklin, Benjamin 28
fraternal lodges 21
funeral procession 21, 78, (*photo*) 79

G

Gothic 3
groceries 60
Gross, Bert (*photo*) 197
growth 121, 142, 160, 169, 173
Grubstake Beer Garden (*photo*) 111
Gunnison (*photo*) 5, 201, 202
Gunnison, Captain John 199
Gunnison County 3, 4

H

hauling mining timber (*photo*) 38
Hayden Survey 4
High Country Citizens Alliance (HCCA) 127, 153
hippies 110, 113, 124
Home Rule 122
Horace Anthracite, *See* Peanut Mine
hot dogger (*photo*) 116
housing 43
hunting (*photo*) 72

I

Industrial Workers of the World, *See* Wobblies
Irwin (*photo*) 36
Italy 10

J

Jackers 19
Joe Block's meat market (*photo*) 75
John's Store 98
Jokerville Mine 203
    explosion 40, 204

K

Keystone Mine and Mill 100, 103, 128, 206
Knights of Pythia Hall (*photo*) 22, 23, (*photo*) 164
Kochevar houses (*photo*) 101
Krizmanich, Johnny 12, 14, 28, 31, 38, 55, 60, 61, 141, 167, 168, 180, (*photo*) 180
Krizmanich, June 111, 181, (*photo*) 181
Ku Klux Klan (KKK) 24, 25
    republican ticket 24
Kuziak, Jim 120, (*photo*) 122

L

language 25, 26, 30
laundry 62, (*photo*) 80
Law-Science Academy 105
lodges 21, 22, 31, 77, 78, (*photo*) 79
Ludlow Massacre 51
Ludlow tent colony (*photo*) 52

M

McNeill, Lyle 119, (*photo*) 120, 131, 166, 167, 156, 184, 184
Malensek, Margaret 67, 68, 117, 183, (*photo*) 183
Malensek, Matt 53, 182, (*photo*) 182
Malensek Ranch 105
Malensek, Rudy 117, 183, (*photo*) 183
Map, Gunnison County 4
Map, Southeastern Europe 10
Masons 22
Memorial Day (*photo*) 152, (*photo*) 153, 154
Metzler, Alberta (*photo*) 27
Metzler, V. E. (*photos*) 69, 76
Metzler, Mrs. V. E. (*photo*) 76
Mihelich, Tony 185, (*photo*) 185
Mitchell, W 127–130, (*photo*) 132, 135
Minersville 200
molybdenum 127, 128, 130, 132, 134, 208
Mountain Bike Hall of Fame 143
mountain biking (*photo*) 117, 141
Mt. Crested Butte 207
Mt. Emmons (*photo*) 128, 130, 133, 208
mule yard (*photo*) 47

N

New Town (*photo*) 43

O

Oh-Be-Joyful 3
Old Rock School 68

P

parades 29, 143
Peanut Mine 33, 36, 37, 44
Pershing 44
pie-cakers 19
Pittsburg 3
post office 163
Poverty Gulch 3
prejudice 18, 20, 24
protesting AMAX (*photo*) 129, (*photo*) 135
public lands 171

R

Rademan, Myles 120, (*photo*) 121
ranching 145, 147
recreation 70
Red Lady Ball (*photo*) 165
religious tolerance 25
Rice, Fred 105
rotary snowplow (*photo*) 86
round-heads 19
Ruby-Irwin 3

S

Saya, Jacob "Jake" (*photo*) 66
Saya, Joe 18, 29, 56, 65, 86, 89, 186, (*photo*) 186
scabs 50
Schmidt, Jim 152
Sedmak, Joe 37, 87, (*photo*) 125, 133, 187, (*photo*) 187
Sedmak, Rudy 21, 35, 49, 188, (*photo*) 188
Seiberling, John (*photo*) 132
shoes of striker's children (*photo*) 54
shot setters 35
shovelling 90
Shuster Band (*photo*) 76

Sibley, George 152
ski area 90, (*photo*) 103, 110, (*photo*) 166, 208
ski bums 107, 116, 118
skiing 88, 89, 91, (*photo*) 142
sleigh riding 88, 89
Slogar Bar (*photos*) 63, 97
Slovenia 10, 11, 12
Smith Hill 44
Smith, Dr. Hurbert Winston 105
Smoke houses 62, 63
Snodgrass Mountain 164, 208
snow 85, 86, 90
    removal 87
"Snowshoers" at Irwin (*photo*) 87
Somrak, Frances 189, (*photo*) 189
Somrak, John 13, 19, 26, 44, 48, 70, 78, 79, 189, (*photo*) 89, 156, 189
Spehar, Betty 22, 77, 151, 190, (*photo*) 190
Sporcich, Gary 153
Sprung, Gary 153, (*photo*) 165
Society of St. Joseph 21
Society of the Blessed Virgin Mary of Perpetual Aid, *also* St. Mary's 23
softball championship (*photo*) 157
St. Patrick's Church 23, 24, (*photo*) 26
Stajduhar, Josephine 68, 69, 81, 97, 110, 112, 140, 191, (*photo*) 191
Stefanic, Eleanor 192, (*photo*) 192
Stefanic's grocery 58
Stefanic, Tony 58, (*photo*) 100, 116, 134, 192, (*photo*) 192
summertime 46
Supply Store 44

T

Tezak, Martin "Teeny" 14, 33, 41, 60, 61, 73, 74, 118, 193, (*photo*) 193
Telluride 169
The Saya family (*photo*) 66
tipple 33
Nelson, Tom (*photo*) 132
tourism 103, 114, 119, 137, 159, 167
town meeting (*photo*) 127
trust fund babies 118

U

unemployment 75
unionization 50, 52, 56
United Mine Workers of America (UMW) 46, 51, 54, 55, 205
United Mine Workers of Colorado (UMW) 51

V

Vandervoort, Sherry (*photo*) 156
Verzuh's Store (*photo*) 59
Vintok Harvest Festival (*photo*) 161

W

Walton, Ralph 106
Washington Gulch 3
Wildflower Festival 143
Wobblies 51, 54

Y

Yaklich, Cindy (*photo*) 195
Yaklich, Fred 24, 36, (*photo*) 104, (*photo*) 105, 194, (*photo*) 194
Yaklich, Leola 195, (*photo*) 195
Yaklich, Trudy (*photo*) 195